# GLIMPSES OF GLORY

*Especially for Branden*

*Ken Hawthorp 10/12/2013*

# GLIMPSES OF GLORY

A Forgotten Pitcher's Journey
To The Bigs And Beyond

By: Ron Gawthorp

Copyright © 2012 by Ron Gawthorp.

| Library of Congress Control Number: | | 2012912666 |
|---|---|---|
| ISBN: | Hardcover | 978-1-4771-4351-3 |
| | Softcover | 978-1-4771-4350-6 |
| | Ebook | 978-1-4771-4352-0 |

All rights reserved. Ronald A. Gawthorp. No part of this book may be reproduced or transmitted in any form or by any means, electronic or mechanical, including photocopying, recording, or by any informational storage or retrieval system—except by a reviewer who may quote brief passages in a review to be printed in a magazine or newspaper—without permission in writing from the author.

This book is a work of non fiction. All persons mentioned are real historical figures. Every effort has been made to verify names, dates, and records of accomplishment. Any errors in reporting this information are unfortunate and every attempt will me made to correct it in future editions. Errors or new information should be sent to the publisher.

Printed in the United States of America

To order additional copies of this book, contact:
Xlibris Corporation
1-888-795-4274
www.Xlibris.com
Orders@Xlibris.com
118960

# CONTENTS

Foreword ..................................................................................... xi

Chapter 1: Savor The Moment ........................................................ 1
Chapter 2: Mysterious Cy ............................................................... 4
Chapter 3: America Circa 1915 ....................................................... 9
Chapter 4: 1916 A Cardinal Tryout ................................................ 16
Chapter 5: A Fort Wayne Chief ..................................................... 20
Chapter 6: 1918 A Season Shortened By War ................................ 30
Chapter 7: The Triple I League ..................................................... 34
Chapter 8: Off To Nashville In A New Era .................................... 41
Chapter 9: Now a Traveler ............................................................ 62
Chapter 10: A Second Chance At The Majors ............................... 66
Chapter 11: A Rookie Senator ....................................................... 82
Chapter 12: Way Down South In Dixie ....................................... 111
Chapter 13: Memphis, Atlanta ..................................................... 115
Chapter 14: New Orleans, Kansas City ........................................ 117
Chapter 15: The 'Little Train' Stops in Omaha ............................ 129

## DEDICATION

*In Memory of Wallace "Cy" Warmoth*
*Who Took The Journey . . .*

*Cy apparently never had a baseball card, so we made him one and put it on the cover of this book. The artist's rendition is a composite of the way he might have looked in his days in Washington. The art is based on the few available news clippings we were able to find. We believe the signature to be very close to the way he signed baseballs for fans.*

## ALSO DEDICATED TO

*For Melvin Briggs, my late father-in-law who planted the seed of this book years ago.*

*And for Gene "Hap" Hulfachor, my great Illinois neighbor and sports loving barber who passed away before I could consult him on this book. He knew more baseball trivia than I could ever write.*

**Special Thanks to:**
**Baseball-Research.com**
**Retrosheet.Org**
**Wikipedia.Org**

**There is an army of volunteers out there, resurrecting The great baseball games of yesteryear**

# A FOREWORD

IN THE EARLY 1970's I first heard about "Cy" Warmoth when my father-in-law said that a man born in Bone Gap, Illinois played baseball for the Washington Senators (Nationals) and he had heard that same man struck out Babe Ruth. He said he did not know it to be true because he had never seen a newspaper clipping to prove it. Melvin Briggs also said he first heard the story as a young man when he too played baseball. The statement excited my curiosity. I rifled some libraries but never found a trace of Wallace Walter "Cy" Warmoth.

Forty years later, retired and back to writing, I discovered large chunks of data about Cy Warmoth on the Internet. He was indeed a professional baseball player of the past. Once only a footnote in Illinois folklore for me, he soon blossomed into a flesh-and-blood southpaw who played among the greats of the game. He fanned Ty Cobb, Babe Ruth and Joe Sewell never dreaming *they* would one day be immortalized in a Baseball Hall of Fame, mainly because it, like the All Star Game, had not yet been born.

Warmoth played baseball before fields had lights and radio announcers called games. He was owned traded and discarded by baseball barons with the same dispatch he delivered curves, sinkers and fastballs.

Following Cy on his quest I began to mentally see baseball as I had never known it. I met flesh and blood men—many branded with colorful nicknames—who had to stand in line to get a cold shower after a ball game. I rode with them on the cheap, sparsely-furnished, dirty railroad coaches provided by their owners. I visited ballparks ranging from majestic (in their day) to old wooden bleachers in a ballpark where the outfield sloped uphill.

Cy Warmoth's journey also exposed me to the inequities of the early game. I saw players bought and sold for sizeable sums of money that often did not translate into a single farthing for the players themselves. Cy would never be a free agent but would always be his own man. Players in Cy's era who didn't go where traded had to miss two years of baseball or find another line of work.

While visiting hundreds of web pages and rifling through countless library books, I beheld the roots, sprouts, and shoots of a still distant baseball "plant" that would one day yield bounty for all involved. I observed trials and errors of the game, steps and missteps, grow into procedures and rules. I beheld rowdy devils, high-strung heroes and nonplussed rubes chasing balls and running bases in every possible venue. I glimpsed the seedy bet hustlers lurking under the grandstands and witnessed spitballers fade away as the pitcher's edge was nipped by the lively ball. I grimaced for the shame of Shoeless Joe and bowed my head at the news of the tragic death of Ray Chapman. Through these insights I also began to understand baseball's long and constant state of evolution. I much better understood how much the pampered stars of today owe those rough and tumble baseball bums of yesteryear.

My host's stay in the majors was short and so he led me elsewhere. He did not quit the majors and quietly go home to hang up his spikes. (And yes they were real spikes.) He went through the minor leagues of the South and then headed out West. While his body allowed, he played baseball in the byways of America. His beginning and end were much the same. In many ways his stops before and after the majors were just as interesting, although less documented, as his stay in "The Bigs". I followed this youthful southpaw from his birthplace in Bone Gap, Illinois to his final stand in Omaha, Nebraska and beheld his many peers that came and went through the revolving door of baseball.

The panorama was excellent. I sensed the exuberance and excess of the roaring twenties and felt the pangs of pain created by the Great Depression. I realized the potential of baseball growth when I beheld ballpark nights were silent and dark. I joined breathless children slipping through holes in wooden fences and ran as fast as little legs would carry me to chase a ball knocked out of the park in hopes of getting a free pass to the next game.

As I watched Cy Warmoth battling through his stations in life, I became the kid watching Babe Ruth through a knothole in a fence. I did all this through the magic of the modern day computer while watching modern baseball games on television. I also found historical baseball moments caught on film and now accessible by computer. When I found a new name I could simply ©Google it and find a picture and known facts. I marveled at the information that has been found and preserved by the "grounds keepers" of this sport. I cannot say enough about the organizations—and countless unpaid volunteers—that live to preserve the records.

Unfortunately not all the records are yet visible. My book turned out to be as much about baseball as Cy Warmoth. Too many of the records of his minor league games and his life are still hidden but I suspect more will be revealed as time marches on. I would hope, in my wildest dreams, I could revise this book with more information and pictures. Warmoth died in 1957 and is buried in Mt. Carmel, Illinois but I hope he would be proud to know that his days in baseball are now revealed. I thank him deeply for having allowed me to follow him more than half a century after his demise.

I apologize to the Washington Senator's fans for calling this team the Nationals. That franchise was sold to Minnesota. I was surprised to find that there was a great deal of confusion about this team's name in the era about which I write. While they were technically *Senators,* the Washington newspapers of the day, and many of the fans, lovingly called them the *Nationals* or *Nats,* so I too used the Nationals name. *Nationals* was an official nickname of the Senators recognized by Major League Baseball.

What began years ago as curiosity for me grew into a mission. I wrote this book realizing it has more outdated facts and statistics than even the best baseball fan can digest. Cy Warmoth made this improbable journey nearly a century ago. There are some who believe that Minor League Baseball will one day have a Hall of Fame. If and when that happens I hope someone will present this little book to the voting committee because I think Wallace Walter Warmoth deserves a full serving of glory and is worthy of inclusion in such a Hall of Fame.

# CHAPTER 1

# Savor The Moment

THE MAGICAL DAY has long since evaporated but it is not so hard to imagine Cy Warmoth once wanting to savor this one very special moment in his life. He had finally come again to the intersection of desire and reality. In other words, his dream had come true.

Babe Ruth, yes the Great Bambino, is upset by being behind in the count to a nobody pitcher like Cy. Ruth did not step out of the batter's box to regroup; it would have been a rare act of contrition for George Herman "Babe" Ruth, the home run king. He did not bow to new pitchers. He devoured them. As he prepared to wind up Warmoth looked at the baseball. Cy noted it was misshapen, scarred and stained. Mothers wouldn't want kids to play with anything this dirty, he mused. Cy glanced around the mammoth stadium again. Fifteen thousand people in one place screaming for Cy to strike out Babe Ruth. And if he failed, there would be boos. The Washington fans were restless after another disappointing season.

Cy looked again at the legend who was alternatively and ceremoniously thumping his spikes and then swinging his bat. Wow, he *was* powerful! No wonder he had hit 59 home runs last year. He swung at every pitch like he wanted to crush the ball. Walter had told Cy that was the secret to striking out Babe Ruth.

Cy smiled at the mere thought that Walter "The Big Train" Johnson had given him, little old nobody Wallace Walter Warmoth, advice on pitching Babe Ruth. Johnson had to be one of the nicest baseball players he had ever met. And what a pitcher! He could throw a baseball so darned hard and he did it nearly sidearm to boot. Walter refused to brush back his hitters by throwing high and inside. "I throw too hard," he said more than once. "If I hit somebody in the head, I'll kill them. I love baseball but I'm not here to kill anyone." All the hitters knew it (and appreciated it) but that made Johnson's accomplishments all the more amazing. Big Train had one less pitch in his arsenal than the other pitchers.

"Cy, he's a one-hundred thousand dollar kitten," Walter had said about Babe, referring to the fact that Yankee owner Colonel Jacob Ruppert had paid Red Sox owner H. Harrison Frazee one hundred thousand dollars and security on a three-hundred thousand loan, for ownership of Ruth.[1]

"Oh darn," Cy muttered. "Here comes Milan. Man, don't take me out today. I've got my stuff today, I know I have." Then he saw catcher Pete Lapan rise from his crouch and also head his way. He put the ball behind his back. If Milan wanted it he would have to take it away from him. The manager saw the subtle move and understood what Cy wanted.

"Relax Wally," the coach said. "I just came out here to help you ice down that million-dollar baby. You've got your stuff today. I plan on leaving you in the whole game. You need a win if I'm going to make a case to keep you here next year. Hell, I need a win. We're 25 games out of first and third from the bottom of the league. Walter Johnson will be here next year but me and you and Pete here," he motioned to the catcher, "we need some insurance. Beating the Yankees this late in the season is always good medicine. If you strike him out, you'll earn yourself a little place in history. Baseball is always going to remember Babe. You can at least say you struck out one of the greatest home run hitters ever. The rest of us will be forgotten."

Lapan chuckled. "Sic him Cy! I think he was out on the town last night. He acts a little woozy."

"It's probably the heat. Babe's a big man and he doesn't handle heat well. He could bunt a ball over that right field wall," Milan said. "If you pitch him low and inside, he'll step back and drop it right on the roof of that house." He was referring to the place in right field where the fence had been diverted towards home plate to accommodate a group of houses the owner had refused to sell to the park owners. "He's already missed high and outside twice. What can we throw him Pete?'

Lapan spat a stream towards first base.

"I think you need to make him reach," the catcher said. "I'm telling you he's got a gut ache. Cy's curve is breaking pretty good today. If he can throw it so it breaks hard outside in the middle of the zone. I think he'll miss it."

Milan looked at Cy.

"What do you think, Cy?"

"He's been squinting pretty bad today," Cy said. "I think he's having trouble following the ball. He held up the dirty brown ball. I think we can sink it low and outside and he'll rip his guts out going after it."

---

[1] http://www.biography.com/people/babe-ruth-9468009

"Up to you, Cy," Milan said adjusting his hat. "Ruth is full of tricks. I'm telling you he knows them all. He's been around the game a long time. He didn't used to stand at bat like that. He picked this stance up from Joe Jackson. Shoeless Joe is all washed up but his batting stance lives on. Ruth is smart. He already knows more about the way you pitch than you do. Look at him and remember it. That squint is probably a trick. Remember he got to the Bigs by pitching.[2] Try it your way one pitch. If it doesn't work, then do whatever Pete says." He turned abruptly and walked to the dug out. Pete headed for home plate. Cy blew air past his lips, making them quiver and producing a horse-like sound.

The ump was screaming:" Play Ball."

The fans were still screaming "Strike him out!"

Babe Ruth, the legend-in-the-making, took a short, hard practice swing and gave Cy a daring smile.

Cy, the southpaw, started his wind up. With all the control and speed he could muster on the brown tattered ball, he sent the orb forward. It curved and dropped. The big batter swung with all the gusto me could muster. The ball smacked the mitt of the catcher with a telling pop. Lapan immediately jumped up and tagged Ruth for safety. Then he turned to Cy and yelled.

"Write home and tell them *you* struck out Babe Ruth!"[3]

"Hey Rookie, that will be the last time." Ruth bellowed. Get yourself a job so I can burn you next year!"

Cy smiled. He would tell them himself. He would get on the train and hurry back to southeastern Illinois and tell them all he had pitched and won a nine-inning game in the major leagues. He would tell them he had struck out Babe Ruth in the last regular season game of 1922.

He just hoped the Nationals would invite him back. God, he loved baseball. He hoped he could play it forever.

---

[2]  http://www.historicbaseball.com/players/j/jackson_joe.html

[3]  This is dramatization based on a box score. The conversations are not known to have taken place. The author put the words in the mouths of the characters!

# CHAPTER 2

# Mysterious Cy

RECENTLY AN EBAY seller who specializes in autographs of the famous and semi-famous offered for sale a autograph of Cy Warmoth. He called it rare and said he had only seen two of them in his career. He said Cy died in obscurity, which maybe is another name for Mt. Carmel, Illinois if you don't know anything about the geography of the United States. He also described Cy as semi-literate, which may or may not be true, but is a pretty unfair thing to say about someone you know nothing about.

If it had been an autographed picture or baseball, I probably would have made the purchase. Cy grew up in a small rural community in Southern Illinois. He would have attended school at a time and place in rural America when he would have attended a country school, probably in the first through eighth grades. For that era and location, he would have been considered to have an average education.

Cy Warmoth is nearly as mysterious to me now as when I began this project but I would consider him a great baseball teacher. Just following him 88 years after his debut, I have learned more about baseball than I ever thought I would know.

If you would go into Mt. Carmel, Illinois today and ask a long-time resident to name two major league baseball pitchers who died in Mt. Carmel, you would probably get one answer: Don Liddle. Donald Eugene Liddle is a celebrated figure in Mt. Carmel. Like Cy, he was a southpaw pitcher and he bounced through the minors for several years. Cy was 23 when he first pitched in a major league game. Don Liddle was 28. To be fair, when Cy pitched his very first real game he was 29 years old. He first pitched in a Major League game in St. Louis in 1916. Cy lasted four innings and was knocked out of the park. When Cy appeared in a Cardinal uniform the minor league farm system was just a ballyhooed idea of Branch Rickey, one of the great architects of modern baseball.

Don Liddle was a product of such a farm system. His pitching skills were being quietly honed in places far from Mt. Carmel, beginning in 1946 when he signed with the Milwaukee Braves as an amateur free agent. His first minor league team was the Auburn, New York Cayugas in the Border League. He moved on growing better and stronger. He played in many of the same Leagues which Cy had played in 30 years before him. Liddle played in just about every rating of league that existed until he was called into big league action by the Milwaukee Braves in 1953. The next year he was playing for the fabled New York Giants and pitched in the first and fourth games of the 1954 World Series. The fourth game was his crowning jewel. Liddle pitched 6-2/3 innings of masterful ball. He was the winning pitcher, although he was helped (saved) by relief pitcher Johnny Antonelli in Cleveland Stadium in front of 78,102 screaming (mostly irate) fans. Cleveland had been the hands-on favorite to win the series. Instead they let the Giants take it away from them in four straight games.

The Indians had won 111 games in the American League to get to the series. Ironically, Liddle became most famous for something that happened in game one and not so much for winning game four. In the bottom of the eighth inning with the scored tied 2-2, Liddle was brought on to help out Sal Maglie, the starting pitcher. The batter up was the slugger Vic Wertz. There were runners on first and second with nobody out. Liddle was told to NOT pitch low and outside to Wertz. His first pitch was a high and inside fast ball. Wertz watched it go past. Wertz bunted the next pitch away. Liddle hurled again catching the outside corner for a strike. The next pitch was high and inside and Wertz tried another bunt and it too went foul. Now they suspected he would not bunt. Liddle tossed a curve outside, a ball. The next pitch was away and up. Wertz swung and drove it deep into center.[4]

What happened next ignited the legend of Willie Mays. The drive of about 440-feet went over his head and he turned and ran back and made the catch over his shoulder with his back to the plate.[5]

The play, broadcast worldwide on television has become one of the most memorable film clips in baseball history. Fans, still today, talk about "The Catch." The 2-2 tie was preserved. In the 10th inning Dusty Rhodes homered with two on to win the game.

Thanks to a film clip preserved now on YouTube© you can actually watch Liddell deliver the pitch that led to "The Catch" that is rated as

---

[4] http://www.baseball-reference.com/players/l/liddldo01.shtml

[5] *Every Pitcher Tells A Story*, Seth Swirsky, Times Books, Div of Random House, pp 122, 123

number 4 in the top plays in baseball history. (http://www.youtube.com/watch?v=7dK6zPbkFnE). In another entitled "Willie Mays Famous Catch, you can actually see Liddle walking to the mound in relief and throwing the famous pitch. (http://www.youtube.com/watch?v=gUK9lG-7HTc&feature=related).

Liddle pitched three seasons in the majors. His final record was 28-18 with 4 saves. In 1957 he went to Omaha and pitched for the Cardinal club there. He may have been in Omaha (Cy's last stop on his baseball minor league career) when Cy died in Mt. Carmel.

Donnie Liddle died in Mt.Carmel, Illinois June 5, 2000 at age 75. He is also buried in Highland Memorial Cemetery in Mt. Carmel. (How many small town cemeteries have two professional baseball pitchers in residence?)

There is no attempt here to compare the pitchers. They lived in different times in the history of baseball and had very different experiences and both made major league history.

I now know *some* of what Cy accomplished in his career in baseball and I am both dazzled and amazed. He is a kid who played with magical giants in a mystical time of baseball in America. Born in the Bone Gap area of Edwards County, Illinois, he almost became a Major League baseball player in1916. He did not last long enough at that job to even be classified as a rookie. His was a short stay in the majors but it must have been magical. When his dance on the big stage ended in 1923, Wally Warmoth kept on playing ball and built up an impressive record in the minors. Wherever he played, he always pitched, so Cy must have had *some stuff.*

My late father-in-law, Melvin Briggs, first brought Cy to my attention back in the 1970's. While visiting the Bone Gap Elevator that he co-owned with his father Grant in the little country town of Bone Gap, Illinois. Melvin, severely crippled by arthritis and confined to doing office work, motioned towards the front counter.

"See that man at the counter," he said more than he asked. "I have always heard that he had a brother who played in the major leagues and he struck out Babe Ruth."

"Really!" I exclaimed in total surprise. "I have never heard of anyone from around here making it that big in the major leagues. What team did he play with?"

"I don't know for sure but I think the Washington Senators. I have never seen a picture or a newspaper but I have heard that since I was a kid," Melvin said.

I failed to find anything in area libraries and then filed the information away and only thought of it from time to time as the years rolled by.

It is only the invention, growth and access to The Internet that allowed me to find out a lot more about the baseball career of Cy Warmoth. Yet much of his life is fogged by the passage of years. Yet even in that fog, I was amazed to learn that Cy Warmoth played among and with the mythical giants of baseball. Men that are legend now were flesh and blood competitors and companions to Cy.

Yet, it was not the lot of Cy (or Wally as those close to him knew him) to have a life at the top. He had a tryout with the St Louis Cardinals in 1916 at age 23. The result was not good and Cy went back to the minor leagues. In 1922, at age 29, he emerged on the Washington Senators/Nationals and stayed there two seasons. While there he accomplished two tasks which will live in baseball history. Then it was back to the minors.

So, I began this journey with very little information. The obituary from an old Mt. Carmel newspaper provided me courtesy of the Wabash County Historical Society.

My clues were:
His name: Wallace Walter Warmoth
His date of birth: February 2, 1893 (Ground Hog Day)
His date of death: June 20, 1957
Place of Burial: Highland Memorial Cemetery, Mt. Carmel, Illinois

This story is not a "whodunit." Nor is it a biography. It is a story of a rural Illinois boy who made a great journey in American life. I do not pretend to have answered all the questions about Cy Warmoth. Too much time has passed to fill in all the blanks. Nor do I pretend to have offered anything new about baseball. What I reveal here is information gleaned elsewhere that answered questions for me and has allowed me to weave a re-creation of the times. Other researchers have done the hard work and I have earnestly tried to recognize them. For that reason I have listed footnotes at the end of each page. If you read and refer to the computer sources you will likely find a picture of the ballplayer being discussed. A simpler way is to bring up Baseball-reference.com and type in the name of the player being discussed. You will then see a picture and statistics on the ballplayer. You can do the same thing on Wikipedia.org and sometimes find out additional information.

I have combined information gleaned from these two sources, plus information from library research (aka good old reading) to put together as complete a picture as I could.

For the record, one of the most difficult decisions was what to call the Washington baseball team. They were known as both the Nationals and the Senators. I had always preferred to call them Senators but as I began reviewing Washington newspaper articles I found that the sports reporters of the time referred to them as the Nationals or "Nats", therefore I have used the same name in this book.

# CHAPTER 3

# America Circa 1915

America was not yet 140 years old in 1915 but an old American Revolutionary veteran touring America would have been amazed if not traumatized. The leap in technology would astound him. Rapid advances in science and engineering were everywhere. George Washington and Ben Franklin would have loved the sternwheelers and riverboats. Now they too were growing extinct. Steam engine locomotives now connected most of America and "rapid" travel made it possible to travel from the Atlantic Ocean to the Pacific Ocean (which they didn't even know about) in a week. America was now industrialized. In fact they had been industrialized so long that their employers gave them extra time off. The Saturday work day had been reduced to noon for many. Instant communication had long been available by the telegraph. Now the entire country was being connected by overhead wires which allowed verbal conversations to be transmitted over a similar wire. Imagine if Paul Revere had been able to phone and warn that the British were coming instead of making that horseback ride.

FIFTY YEARS HAD passed since the end of the Civil War. Veterans of that conflict between states North and South still roamed the land, and it was those veterans who first began to make baseball the American passion. It had been a behind-the-lines pastime for both sides.

Slavery had ended but segregation had not. *Jim Crow* ruled the world. Even in the abolition strongholds of the north rules and facilities were separate. This included even the great game of baseball. Professional and minor leagues existed for both black and whites. But it was the white leagues where prosperity *usually* existed. Still men of both races unabashedly played. Baseball offered joy to both fans and players. Rich and poor people, regardless of color, loved baseball. It would be more than 30 years before the major leagues would open up to all talent.

The primary methods of communication in 1915 were newspapers, mail and word of mouth. Penmanship was still an important part of education. Urgent communications were sent via the telegraph, usually at a railroad station. Radio had been invented but was only used by amateurs. At least it would be until the advent and passing of World War I. With the outbreak of war, the U.S. government would shut down public access to radio hobbyists and scientists and try to hustle the young practitioners of the science into the military service. The potential uses of the science of radio were already being realized by generals and admirals. It would be five years before the first commercial radio station would begin broadcasting professional baseball games. Station KDKA of Pittsburgh would be the first to do so.

The primary means of long-distance transportation across land was now the train. It was possible to zigzag the country and reach most of the small cities and towns via the tentacles of the railroad tracks. Personal transportation was being transformed with Henry Ford's mass production of the automobile. If one visited rural America, he could still expect to encounter the horse and buggies but such monstrosities as trucks and tractors were beginning to appear. Major League teams traveled city to city via private coaches which could be attached to scheduled trains. Some owners provided nothing more elaborate than a pot bellied coal stove and hard back chairs. It was pretty much believed to be bad business to baby a ballplayer.

Church and religion were still a force in America, dominated primarily by Christians and Jews. In many communities serious debates flared over whether or not baseball games should be played on Sunday. Branch Rickey, one of the most influential men in professional baseball, would not attend Sunday games. He was office manager of the St. Louis Cardinals. America, still mending itself from Civil War, was wrapped up in an industrial revolution which put the country on the edge of both ecstasy and tragedy. In 1918 professional baseball would stutter-step because of entry into World War I. Later, when the soldiers came home, America would be caught in a whirlwind of new found prosperity. Historians would refer to it as "The Roaring Twenties." And then would follow, almost without warning, "The Great Depression."

Exactly how Wally Warmoth came to love and learn baseball is lost to time. It could have been anywhere because baseball teams were virtually everywhere. There were sandlot teams in every large, medium and small city. There were cow-pasture teams in nearly every rural community.

Factories fielded teams, railroads fielded teams. Churches had teams. It seemed everyone had a team to which they could be faithful.

Author Harold Seymour called the phenomenon of employers fostering baseball to help pacify its employees as "paternalism." Managers, especially those in company towns, felt that it was beneficial to provide sports activities to waylay drunkenness and absenteeism. The Pullman Palace Car Company had such a town on Calumet Lake near Chicago. The company sponsored intramural baseball as well as several traveling teams. The employees lived in company houses and Pullman collected rent from them. A few years after the idea's inception in 1883 the employees futilely struck for an eight-hour workday. In 1894 employees struck again. Pullman refused to negotiate and National Guard and federal troops were dispatched. Thirteen men were killed, including some out playing baseball. The story underlines the American workers' transforming need for leisure and recreation.[6].

Generally baseball was a happy time and wherever 18 or more boys populated a diamond of any sort, a crowd gathered to cheer. Baseball was a rage America had seldom known before. It had the thrill of a gold rush but was available to all. A skill in pitching, hitting, throwing or stealing bases became a gift to be envied. It could mean more. The giants of the game were growing into godliness. Graven images of the giants of the game appeared across the land.

The first such images were called "trade cards". They were simply pictures of a locally famous team pictured on one side of a cardboard, and on the other side an advertisement for almost any business or their wares. Trade cards were popular into the 1880's when tobacco cards began to test their commercial value. Famous players and personalities appeared on the cards. If you collected coupons from your favorite tobacco product and mailed them back to the company, they would send you a card with a picture of a baseball titan on it.

Tobacco companies, present in the U.S. since the founding of the first settlements in Virginia, flourished. Kids demanded cards and adults provided them by buying more and more tobacco products. Some candy products also used miniature cards.

The tobacco business was so good new companies sprang up. The American Tobacco Company began acquiring profitable upstarts and soon

---

[6]   Baseball, The People's Game, Harold Seymour, Oxford University Press, New York, 1999 page 219

ATC grew into a monopoly. Ironically, once American Tobacco reached monopoly status, it saw no need to give away the cards to build sales. Why spend money on baseball cards when they already had most of the business? So from about 1890 to the early 1900's tobacco cards were produced in smaller numbers. A few other businesses tried to capitalize on the void but had nowhere near the widespread distribution power of their predecessors.

Ironically, at least from our view of a current federal government that hates and penalizes tobacco, it was the trustbusters who put tobacco cards back in the hands of children. President Teddy Roosevelt, self-appointed trustbuster, helped break up the American Tobacco Company into several smaller and competing companies. We saw much the same thing last century when the government broke up AT&T. The new competitors went after each other with a vengeance and baseball trading cards with colored pictures of players were the result.

By 1915 Cracker Jack© had entered the fray. The golden era of trading cards had begun. Cracker Jacks, an American staple now, began business in 1896. AuctionLinc (auctionbytes.com) best summarized the Cracker Jack phenomenon as relates to baseball:

> By the time Sailor Jack and his dog Bingo became mascots in 1918, the company had already issued its most valuable prizes: 144 baseball cards featuring the likes of "Shoeless" Joe Jackson, Ty Cobb, and Christy Mathewson. In 2004, a complete set in near mint condition sold at auction for a record $800,000!"

For the original AP news story and for more details about the cards themselves go to CBS SportsLine (http://cbs.sportsline.com/mlb/story/7946720) and Sportscard Guaranty, LLC(http://www.sgc1914crackerjack.com/find.html):[7]

Later baseball trading cards would fall into the hands of the bubble gum manufacturers.

And yes, Virginia, by 1915 there was a Major League. In fact there was more than one. Let's review, thanks again to Baseball-refence.com.

**The National League of 1915** (in their order of finish) consisted of eight teams:

---

[7] http://www.auctionbytes.com/cab/abu/y205/m08/abu0148/s06  Auction Bytes, The Independent Trade Publication For Online Merchants.

1. The Philadelphia Phillies
2. The Boston Braves
3. The Brooklyn Robins
4. The Chicago Cubs
5. The Pittsburg Pirates
6. The St. Louis Cardinals
7. The Cincinnati Redlegs
8. The New York Giants

**The American League of 1915** (in their order of finish) also consisted of eight teams:

1. The Boston Red Sox
2. The Detroit Tigers
3. The Chicago White Sox
4. The Washington Nationals/Senators
5. The New York Yankees
6. The St. Louis Browns
7. The Cleveland Indians
8. The Philadelphia Athletics

In fact, a third major league had been born in 1914 and was still operational in 1915. It was called the Federal League. The members of that league were:

1. The Baltimore Terrapins
2. The Boston Tip-Tops
3. The Buffalo Buffeds/Blues
4. The Chicago Whales/Feds
5. The Indianapolis Hoosiers (would move to New Jersey)
6. The Kansas City Packers
7. The Pittsburgh Rebels
8. The St. Louis Terriers

The Federal League would go broke and cease to exist, mostly due to large court delays which may have involved some skullduggery precipitated by the American and National League owners.

The Boston Red Sox easily won the World Series that year, 4 games to 1. It is an interesting footnote to that series that the Red Sox had especially strong pitching. It was so strong that Sox Manager Bill Carrigan decided not to use a 20-year old who had won 18 regular season games for them, pitching 217 innings. The kid had also hit 29 homers, so Carrigan did put Babe Ruth in one game as a pinch hitter. The time was nearing when a trade of Ruth to the New York Yankees would create the greatest rivalry in Baseball, and reverberate through the baseball ages. Another irony also loomed; in just four years there would be a scandal that would shake the foundation of the sport. It would be called the infamous "Black Sox" Scandal of 1919. Cheating in baseball! It was almost unfathomable.

There were many other leagues that were almost professional but not major. They included:

1. Appalachian League
2. Arizona League
3. California League
4. Carolina League
5. Dominican Summer League
6. Eastern League
7. Florida State League
8. Gulf Coast League
9. International League
10. Mexican League
11. Midwest League
12. New York-Penn League
13. Northwest League
14. Pacific Coast League
15. Pioneer League
16. South Atlantic League
17. Southern League
18. Texas League
19. Venezuelan Summer League[8]

There also existed "The Negro Leagues," just as vibrant and thriving as those in White Leagues, but most not nearly as profitable.

---

[8]   http://web.minorleaguebaseball.com/index.jsp?sid=l120

This then is a snapshot of major and minor league baseball and America in 1915.

It is onto this stage that "Cy" Warmoth stepped in the waning season of 1916. We are uncertain how he came to the threshold of professional baseball. It was said in his obituary that he played with a team called the Indians. His coach was named as Thebe Wirth. The name rings no bells in professional baseball. Cy, mindful of the young pitcher in the movie "The Natural", had been discovered and summoned for a tryout. The previously mentioned Branch Rickey had Cardinal scouts everywhere. Rickey was trying to develop young players before the wealthier Eastern teams could find and sign them. Rickey was working especially close with minor league club owners. He was experimenting with an idea he had to develop farm clubs for young players. Under his plan the players would be signed by the Cardinals and then sent to farm clubs for development.

The Cardinals had another trick for raising funds. They would send out exhibition teams to play against community baseball teams. They would snag one or two of their headline players and send them out into the pasturelands. Meanwhile the Cardinals were playing their regular Major League schedule. It could be that Cy was being considered for—perhaps even played for or against—this team. Someone thought he had talent.

## CHAPTER 4

# 1916
# A Cardinal Tryout

CY WARMOTH LIKELY got his first glimpse of glory on August 31, 1916. That was the day he donned a Cardinal uniform and walked to the pitcher's mound at Robison Field. He was 23 years old and he was probably amazed and proud for the opportunity. Details of the game are sketchy, but he would find his taste of glory bitter. He was not a "real" cardinal. He didn't even qualify as a rookie. He was here for a tryout. It was common practice in baseball in the early 1900's to "sneak" pitchers into the game for a few innings to see how they performed under true game conditions. The further away from first place the team was, the more likely it was a tryout could be arranged; especially if the bull pen had a sag in it. That was certainly the Cardinal situation in the fall of 1916.

The Cardinals were loaded with talent but the season ranked as a disaster. The day Cy took the mound in the fifth inning, the Cardinals had only won 55 games. Only the luckless Cincinnati Reds had lost more in the National League. Making it worse, the cross town rivals, the St. Louis Browns, were playing better than .500 ball and were only 4 games out of first place in the rival American League. There was fan talk of the desirability of consolidating the two teams. It was a rumor that always struck fear in the hearts of players who already had a job. It would be 1954 when the rumors went away forever. That year the Browns moved to Baltimore and became the Baltimore Orioles.

The good news for Cy on August 31 was simply that he could not greatly damage the team's fortunes and he had no reputation to lose. If he did well, he could carve out a place for himself in the National League. If he did poorly, the world of St. Louis baseball would soon forget him.

In 1916 St. Louis was still, and had long been, a hotbed of baseball. Change was constant. Owners, as well as players, came and went like summer breezes. Robison Field had been enlarged to seat 19,000 spectators in 1909. The ballpark became simply **League Park** under new club owners Frank and Emmet Stanley Robison in 1899, a name it bore through 1910.[9] The name of the ballpark was changed to **Robison Field** by Helene Hathaway Britton, owner of the Cardinals, as a memorial to her father, Frank Robison, who died in 1908 and uncle, Stanley Robison who died in 1911. The team and stadium ownership passed to her when her uncle died.[10] The stadium would never know night baseball and was never outfitted with lights.

**Manager Miller (Mighty Mite) Huggins** must have been a little taken aback when he first saw Cy Warmoth. He had asked the front office for another southpaw but he wasn't sure that Warmoth was what he needed. The twenty-three-year-old was a wiry five-feet-ten and probably weighed 160 pounds soaking wet. As mentioned earlier, he was a southpaw, a left handed pitcher. Of course next to the jockey-like stature of Huggins, Cy would have seemed huge.

Trying out for a major league baseball team in early 20$^{th}$ Century America was not an enviable task. When a new guy was successful and won a spot on a team, someone else went home. Those who had already won uniforms would not make it easy for others to enter. They would protect their exclusive memberships every way possible. The only way into the club was to overcome all obstacles. Excellence in baseball discipline was required. A tryout pitcher might be saddled with a catcher who called for pitches he knew opposing batters could hit. A tryout catcher might find himself scrambling for low and outside pitches. In reality a player trying out was probably on better terms with the opposing team than his own comrades. Yet that was a rule only to a point. Baseball players and coaches admired talent and wanted to win. Eventually true talent would be recognized. Ty Cobb discussed his troubles of acceptance during his rookie season in his autobiography.

One of the exciting things about writing about people 94 years after the fact is that you know things they did not know. Nobody knew where this baseball thing was going. There seemed to be a good chance organized baseball could fail financially. Very few of the owners had deep pockets. Their main source of income was selling tickets to baseball games. The second source of cash, mostly reserved for emergencies, was selling players. If you needed a lot of cash, sell a good player. That is how Babe Ruth came to be a Yankee. Probably no 1916 baseball owner would have guessed someday it would be possible to sell as many tickets for night games as day

---

[9] http://en.wikipedia.org/wiki/Robison_Field
[10] http://en.wikipedia.org/wiki/Robison_Field

games. Since television was not yet invented, they certainly wouldn't have suspected what television rights could do for the balance sheet. It would be during the depression days that All Star Games and a Baseball Hall of Fame were contrived. Miller Huggins had no idea he would one day be enshrined in a Baseball Hall of Fame and that he would go from this ragtag outfit in St. Louis to managing the New York Yankees. Huggins became a Hall of Famer in 1964[11]. He was but the first of many famous people Cy would meet in his baseball days. Another hall-of-famer-to-be normally played on the Cardinals team. It was the legendary hitter Rogers Hornsby, but he was not in the game today. Milt Stock was in the lineup in his place. Hornsby, sidelined today, felt he was a great hitter. He was right. Later in his career Hornsby, told a reporter:

"I don't like to sound egotistical, but every time I stepped up to the plate with a bat in my hands, I couldn't help but feel sorry for the pitcher."[12]

Hornsby eventually gained fame in the major leagues but his beginnings were meager and it is through an interview that Hornsby gave to Look magazine and written by J. Roy Stockton that we find out how and why Cy may have found his way onto the Cardinal team.

The article was titled: "How To Get Fired." Hornsby hit the major leagues in 1915, hailing from the small town of Winters, Texas. He started out in Class B ball in Dallas, thanks to a tryout arranged by his older brother. He failed in that tryout because he was too small and was sent to Hugo, Oklahoma to play in the Class D Texas-Oklahoma League. The team was visited by a Cardinals scout named Bob Connery who was in charge of the St. Louis Cardinals "second" team, playing exhibition games.

"In those days," Hornsby told Stockton, "the Cardinals were a poor club, compared to some controlled by wealthy men in larger cities. The only big crowds were on Sundays and during the deciding days of a pennant race. So the Cardinals booked exhibition games on every available day. The club picked up a few thousand dollars extra that way.."[13]

This could explain why Cy Warmoth was listed on the roster of the Cardinals for the entire year, yet only pitched in one game. Exhibition games were common and even the great Babe Ruth participated in two and three-inning exhibition games in the off season. In one such game he

---

[11] http://www.baseball-reference.com/players/h/huggimi01.shtml
[12] http://www.rogershornsby.com/quotes.htm
[13] The Fireside Book of Baseball, Simon and Schuster 1956, pp 196, 197, originally published in *Look* 1953

was struck out by a young woman named Jackie Mitchell. She had just been signed as a pitcher for the Chattanooga Lookouts five days before the exhibition game of April 2, 1931 and because she also struck out Lou Gehrig in the same game, there have always been suspicions of this being a publicity stunt. You can see some of the strikeout on YouTube©.

Exhibition games in the south led to what eventually became Spring Training for baseball major leaguers.

There were other types of baseball exhibitions as well. Many of the most famous of the African American ball players became "barnstormers" and put on exhibition games in the United States, Mexico and South America. The most famous of these "performers" was Satchel Paige who eventually got into major league baseball and is now in the Baseball Hall of Fame.

Paige and Josh Gibson became so legendary as barnstormers that many legendary white players, including Dizzy Dean, a 30-game winner for the St. Louis Cardinals in 1934, wanted to play against the Paige All Stars. Not long after his victorious season had ended, Dizzy Dean struck out 15 of the All Stars and gave up only one run. Paige pitched 13 innings of nearly perfect ball and allowed no runs. Afterwards Dean acknowledged Paige as "the best pitcher in the business."[14]

We are uncertain why Cy's career with the St. Louis Cardinals is listed as it is, but while he had had his first glimpse of glory there, his pitching was anything but spectacular. In five innings he gave up 10 runs in a situation where he should have expected to give up two. He had no hits but did participate in one put out.

Cy may have been excited by what he saw and heard, but he could not have been proud of the way he played and probably headed home with his chin in the mud. He'd had his big chance and muffed it. But Cy had a much longer baseball road ahead of him than he knew.

AUTHORS NOTE: Most records indicate Cy appeared in three Cardinals game but the author has been unable to find specific records of other appearances.

---

[14] The Fireside Book of Baseball, Simon and Schuster, 1956 pp 85

# CHAPTER 5

# A Fort Wayne Chief

CY DISAPPEARS AFTER the 1916 season. He likely went somewhere and went to work. His obituary listed him as a switchman on the New York Central railroad. We have no idea when or where he went to work for the railroad but we have already established that railroads were big proponents of baseball. Or, he may have gone back to the farm in Illinois.

It is interesting to compare the plight of Cy Warmoth with that of Rogers Hornsby who got his Cardinal tryout just one year earlier. One would assume that Hornsby emerged from obscurity and rocketed to greatness. That was not quite the case. St. Louis paid his Oklahoma team $400 to send him to St. Louis. Hornsby got nothing for moving up. Hornsby joined the Cardinals in September 1915 and at the end of the season Manager Miller Huggins told the future Hall of Famer (and remember Huggins was also headed there) who had hit a mere .246 in 18 games:

> "You're too little kid. Those strong-armed pitchers in the big leagues will handcuff you. You ought to be farmed out until you put one some weight."
>
> "I was just a green country kid from Texas," Hornsby recalled, "and to me farming out meant just that. I didn't know about any farm system in baseball. In fact, we didn't have anything like that in those days. It was just a way of expressing himself that Huggins used. So I literally did what I thought he meant. I arranged to spend the winter on a farm with an aunt and uncle. I drank all the milk I could hold and consumed great piles of fried chicken and dozens of homemade biscuits every day.[15]

---

[15] The Fireside Book of Baseball, Simon and Schuster 1956, pp 196, 197, originally published in *Look* 1953

Hornsby reported back to Huggins in the spring weighing 160 pounds. If Huggins was that hard on Hornsby, it is not hard to imagine what he said to Cy.

Wherever he was, Cy undoubtedly followed the games of the 1916 World Series. The Series featured the American League's Boston Red Sox against the Brooklyn Dodgers. The series opened in Boston at Braves Field with an attendance of 36,117. Since radio was invented but not yet utilized for news, weather and sports, he would had to follow it by newspaper and possibly getting some early results from a friendly telegraph operator.

The news flashes between telegraph operators could have gone like this:

NO SCORE IN FIRST
STOP
NO SCORE IN SECOND
STOP
HUBIZEL TRIPLES STOP LEWIS DOUBLE DRIVES HIM IN
STOP
SCORE ONE ZERO BOSTON AHEAD
STOP
FOURTH NO SCORE BOSTON
STOP
STENGEL SCORES ON WHEAT TRIPLE
STOP

GAME TIED AT ONE
STOP
FIFTH HOOPER SCORES ON MARQUARD TRIPLE
STOP
BOSTON AHEAD TWO TO ONE
STOP
SIXTH NO SCORE
STOP
BOSTON LEAD TWO TO ONE
STOP
SEVENTH SOX EXPLODE SCORE THREE
STOP
BOSTON UP FIVE TO ONE
STOP

EIGHTH BOSTON SCORES ANOTHER
STOP
NOW SIX ONE
STOP
ROBINS POST FOUR RUNS IN NINTH BUT LOSE GAME
TO BOSTON SIX TO FIVE
STOP

Boston went on to win the World Series in five games. Brooklyn did manage to win the third game 6 to 5. As is usual for American baseball there were some interesting characters in this series. Some of these players would also be Hall of Famers.

Perhaps most notable was Charles Dillon "Casey" Stengel. Stengel traveled a path to the majors that mirrored many of the stops Cy Warmoth would make in his final years. Casey's tour of backroads America included work with the Kansas City Blues and smaller teams in Kankakee, Illinois and Shelbyville and Maysville, Kentucky. In 1912 he landed a position with the team that would become the Brooklyn Dodgers and posted an astounding .312 average. He demanded a $2,100 per year contact from the Dodgers and got it. The next year he became the first ball player to hit a home run out of Ebbet's Field but his batting average fell to .272. In 1917 he was traded to the Pittsburgh Pirates and played for 39 games before leaving to serve when America entered World War I. In 1919 he came back to the Pirates, was traded to the Philadelphia Athletics whom he didn't like. He eventually got the trade rescinded and a trade made to the New York Giants instead.

Before baseball Stengel had been a dentist in his hometown of Kansas City. His comical antics as a player and a manager will live in baseball stories forever.[16] He once put a pigeon in his hat and when arguing with an umpire tipped his hat and let the bird fly away. Of course, it cracked up the crowd.

Another interesting character in the 1916 series was John Tortes "Chief" Meyers a Dartmouth educated Cahuilla Indian. He played in four World Series games but his perhaps best known as the catcher for the seemingly immortal Christy Mathewson, a Hall of Fame pitcher.

There was a Cameo appearance in the series for the Sox. George Herman "Babe" Ruth pitched a 14-inning game two and allowed six hits and one

---

[16] http://www.caseystengel.com/bio.htm

run against his team. Some were excited about his prospects. However he didn't have much luck at hitting. Ruth did have a run batted in (RBI).

Cy does not reappear in official baseball records until 1917 when he called the *Grand Duchess* of Fort Wayne, Indiana his new home. One does not normally associate Fort Wayne with the big leagues of American sports but it has an impressive history. One of the more surprising facts is that the professional basketball team, *The Detroit Pistons,* was actually relocated from Fort Wayne to Detroit in 1957. The team was begun by Foundry Owner Fred Zollner, whose foundry was famous for manufacturing pistons for railroad, truck and car engines. In Fort Wayne the team played in the Basketball Association of America. Zollner himself relocated the team to Detroit which had lost its only professional basketball team a decade earlier. The *Pistons* had been involved in a never-proven point shaving controversy in the middle fifties while in Fort Wayne but the main reason for the move was that the city was not large enough to continually support a pro sports team in the modern era.[17]

Cy Warmoth signed to play for the Fort Wayne Chiefs in the Central League. The League was listed as a "Class B" team in 1917. The other teams in the League were:

- Dayton Veterans
- Evansville Evas
- Grand Rapids Black Sox
- Muskegon Muskies
- Richmond Quakers
- South Bend/Peoria Benders/Distillers
- Springfield Reapers

Oddly there are no references to the Fort Wayne Chiefs in the city's sports history. The league may have been more of an industrial league team. Regardless of its origins, it is a league that sent many players to the majors. One of the more notable was Stanley Raymond "Bucky" Harris of the Muskegon Muskies. Although Harris was gone from the Central League in 1917, Cy would be his teammate on the Washington Nationals in 1922 and 1923. Bucky was destined to be a key player in one of the ten greatest games in baseball history in 1924.

---

[17] http://en.wikipedia.org/wiki/Fort_Wayne_Pistons

One of the fascinating things about professional baseball in this era is the amount of traffic to and from the major leagues. This was possible because of something called "the reserve clause." Simply stated, professional baseball controlled a player's professional life and destiny once he signed a contract. All contracts were for a one year period. At the end of the year it was time to renegotiate the contract. A player had to accept what his "owner" offered him or not sign and be out of professional baseball. (The ban was good for one year plus another year if a player didn't re-sign.) Star players had some negotiating power but most players did not. The owners developed the system to hold down salaries and it worked. The player was owned, much like a slave. The owner had the right to buy, sell or trade him without considering the desires of the player. The Sherman Anti-Trust Act of 1890 prohibited such collusion between interstate industries. Baseball, the Supreme Court ruled in 1922, was merely an amusement and not subject to interstate commerce regulation. The ruling is still in effect today.[18]

When professional ballplayers were finally able to organize a union, and this caused a lot of strife and division, things began to change. It was not until 1974 that things turned around dramatically. Oakland Athletics Owner Charles Finley refused to make an annuity payment to Catfish Hunter as required in a contract he had signed. Marvin Miller, attorney for the Major League Baseball Players Association, had previously been able to win a collective bargaining agreement with owners in 1968. That agreement provided for using arbitrators when team owners and players had contract disputes. Before the agreement impasses were broken by the Baseball Commissioner. The commissioner was hired and paid by the team owners. Arbitration of the Catfish Hunter and Oakland Athletics dispute resulted in the arbitrator deciding that Catfish Hunters contract had been violated and therefore was no longer in effect. Catfish Hunter was declared a free agent and then signed a five-year, $3.5 million agreement with the New York Yankees. Players immediately saw how much money could be made in professional baseball.[19]

But in 1917 the owners controlled every aspect of their game, including the commissioner. They even got the lion's share of the revenue created by baseball cards.

---

[18] http://en.wikipedia.org/wiki/Reserve_clause#History_and_baseball

[19] http://en.wikipedia.org/wiki/Marvin_Miller

The Fort Wayne Team, like every other minor league team in baseball, had several players either coming from or going to the majors. They included:

- Manager **Carl Vandagrift**,[20] Indianapolis Hoosiers* of the 1914 Federal League
- **Frank Rooney,** Indianapolis Hoosiers of the 1914 Federal League.[21]
- **Ralph Miller,** played shortstop for the Philadelphia Athletics in 1920 and 1921 and then was traded to the Washington Nationals and would join **Bucky Harris** in the great World Series of 1924.[22]
- **Frank Gleich,** became a Yankee Outfield in 1919-1920[23]
- Finally there was **Tex Hoffman** who played third base for Cleveland in 1915 and then returned to the minors. Like Cy, he played in the minors for many years and lived in many states and towns[24].

The career of Cy Warmoth crossed many of the meridians of baseball's growth and transition. In 1913 a group of investors, mostly industrialists, formed to purchase an independent minor league called the Columbia League. Quickly it changed its name to the Federal League. In 1914 the industrialist owners included Harry F. Sinclair of Sinclair Oil, Phillip Ball, who owned the St. Louis Browns and was an ice magnate besides, and George S. Ward of the Ward Baking Company. This was a major challenge to the two leagues of major league baseball. John T. Powers started out as head of the league but he was replaced soon after. Under the new leadership of James A. Gilmore the league declared itself a major league and began luring American and National League players with signing bonuses.

The Federal League consisted of eight teams. Four were placed in big cities and the other four, Indianapolis being one of them, in small metropolitan areas. The locations were Chicago, St. Louis, Pittsburgh, Brooklyn, Baltimore, Buffalo, Indianapolis and Kansas City.[25]

---

[20] http://www.baseball-reference.com/minors/player.cgi?id=vandag001car
[21] http://www.baseball-reference.com/players/r/roonefr01.shtml
[22] http://www.baseball-reference.com/players/m/millera03.shtml
[23] http://www.baseball-reference.com/players/g/gleicfr01.shtml
[24] http://www.baseball-reference.com/players/h/hoffmte01.shtml
[25] http://en.wikipedia.org/wiki/Federal_League

Several players, including **Walter Johnson** of the Washington Nationals/Senators signed Federal League contracts and a few actually went and played for the organization. The Washington owners were finally able to convince Johnson to stay in the American League. The Federal League threat ended in 1915 when a judge ruled that Major League Baseball was exempt from Sherman Anti Trust Act.[26] What is really interesting is how this matter was resolved and what resulted. The Federal League originally filed the lawsuit claiming the American and National Leagues were in violation of the anti-trust provisions. The Federal League won its case and the leagues were ordered to pay damages of nearly $250,000. The other leagues appealed and won the appeal. The Supreme Court finally ruled in 1922, in an opinion written by Justice Oliver Wendell Holmes, Jr., that baseball was not subject to Interstate Commerce. In the meantime the Federal League had gone broke waiting on a decision.

The Federal League might have been able to weather the storm financially had it not been for the delays caused by Federal Judge Kenesaw (sic) Mountain Landis of Ohio. (He was named for the Mountain in Georgia where his father lost a leg in the Civil War. The battle site was actually spelled Kennesaw Mountain and it was erroneously recorded on his birth certificate). More interestingly, Landis, an ardent baseball fan, did not rule immediately on the appeal. He urged the three leagues to negotiate. This period of delay cost the Federal League and their team owners immensely.[27]

Later Judge Landis became the First Major League Commissioner of Baseball in 1919, not long after the infamous Black Sox Scandal rocked baseball to its foundation.

Baseball has one last tribute to the Federal League. Weeghman Park was build for Chicago's Federal Team, The Whales. Later it came into possession of a chewing gum manufacturer named Wrigley. Now you know the park as Wrigley Field, home of the Chicago Cubs.[28]

Baseball was growing in many ways and the growth pains were both exciting and troubling to its players. While players had not really unionized, they surely were organizing. Players like Cy Warmoth had both minor and major league networks to help him in his career.

---

[26] http://en.wikipedia.org/wiki/Federal_Baseball_Club_v._National_League
[27] http://en.wikipedia.org/wiki/Kenesaw_Mountain_Landis
[28] http://en.wikipedia.org/wiki/Federal_League

If the players thought they were already troubled, they were unknowingly sitting on the cusp of other great changes. The drums of war in Europe had long been beating and on April 6, 1917 America entered the war on the sides of her allies, Russia, France and England.

As mentioned earlier not much is known about the "Fort Wayne Indians". The ball park, The Grand Duchess, was an elaborate minor league facility, perhaps modeled after one by the same name in Cincinnati. The Native American theme reverberated around Fort Wayne for many years. The very first professional team was the 1871 Kekiongas. Apparently things didn't go well. Several of the players, most of them from Baltimore, took advances on their wages and then skipped town while the season was still underway.[29] Two of the remaining players got arrested for public drunkenness and that pretty much ended Fort Wayne's foray into professional baseball.

In 1882 and 1883 an unclassified team called the Fort Wayne Hoosiers played in the Northwestern League. The league roster looked similar to the league Cy would play in. Along with the Indians, teams from Bay City and Grand Rapids, Michigan, three Illinois teams (Quincy, Springfield and Peoria) plus the Toledo, Ohio Blue Stockings comprised the league. The Hoosiers were the first team that recorded the Grand Duchess as their home stadium.

In 1896 a Class C Minor League team called the Fort Wayne Farmers appeared at the Duchess. In addition to the Farmers, the Interstate League of which they were members, included: The Jackson Wolverines, The New Castle Salamanders, the Saginaw Lumbermen, the Toledo Mud Hens (later made famous by the M*A*S*H television show), the Washington D.C. Little Nationals, the Wheeling West Virginia Nailers and the Youngstown, Ohio Puddlers. No records could be found for these games.

In 1897 the Interstate League had raised its rating to Class B and the Fort Wayne team had changed its name from Farmers to Indians. This year the Mansfield Ohio Haymakers were in and the Little Nationals were not. The Salamanders changed their name to Quakers. The Interstate League was stable at Class B until 1901 when suddenly it became the Fort Wayne Railroaders and the League changed to the Western Association and the rating was changed to Class A.[30] Teams came joined and vanished or changed names. Several names changed and the most notable was that the Toledo team had now become the Swamp Angels.

---

[29] http://www.baseball-reference.com/bullpen/1871_Kekiongas
[30] http://www.baseball-reference.com/minors/league.cgi?id=14541

The Fort Wayne Railroaders played until 1905, a year they shared a team with the Canton Red Stockings. In 1906 they were listed as only Fort Wayne and were back in the Interstate League, which had a Class C rating. No team was listed for 1907. In 1908 through 1910 (three seasons) the Fort Wayne Team called itself the Bilikens and they were in the Central League. The Central League still consisted of eight teams and had a Class B rating. One of the newcomers to the League was the Evansville (Indiana) River Rats baseball team. They would later become the Evas and Cy would play for them. In 1911 the Fort Wayne team changed its name yet again. It was now called the "Brakies." In 1912 they were again The Railroaders. In 1913 yet another name change, they were called The Champs, in 1914 they were again The Railroaders but in 1915 they were the Fort Wayne Cubs. All of these teams played their games in the Grand Duchess Stadium.

In 1916 there was no team. This brings us to 1917, the year after Cy's failed tryout for the Cardinals. His team was the Fort Wayne Chiefs. The League was still rated Class B and, as mentioned earlier, the team was loaded with talent. Based on records available, Cy pitched 50 innings in six games. He won 2 and lost 4. This may not be an accurate accounting, however. Fort Wayne and the Grand Duchess were going through hard times. When the 1917 season closed there would be no more minor league baseball in Fort Wayne until 1928. By then the league had dropped to six teams but it still retained its Class B rating.

# Elsewhere in Baseball

## THE DOUBLE NO HITTER

Perhaps the biggest baseball story in 1917 was an epic no hitter battle between The Cincinnati Reds and the Chicago Cubs at Weeghman Park (Wrigley Field) on May 2.

Jim Vaughn of the Reds and Cubs Pitcher Fred Toney pitched flawless ball for nine innings. The score was tied 0-0 at the end of nine innings.

It ended in the tenth when Larry Kopf of the Reds drilled the ball to right center for a single. The double no-hitter ended. Hal Chase followed with another fly to center. Outfielder Cy Williams got both hands on it but dropped it anyway. Kopf went all the way to third.

The game was sealed when a tired old footballer, trying to make a new career in baseball hit a swinging bunt to third. Pitcher Vaughn fielded the ball and knew he did not have a chance to throw out Jim Thorpe who was streaking to first base.

"He was still fast as a race horse," Vaughn recalled in an interview with Hal Totten. He turned his attention elsewhere.

"I scooped it towards home plate," Vaughn said. "I did not realize Kopf was right behind me. I could have turned around and tagged him out." Catcher Art Wilson seemed paralyzed and the ball hit him in the chest protector and dropped to the ground.

"I looked over my shoulder and saw Chase round third," Vaughn recalled. He yelled to the catcher.

"Are you going to let him score too?" Wilson snapped out of it grabbed the ball and tagged out the runner."

The Cubs pitcher recalled things were tense in the clubhouse afterwards. Wilson, he remembered, cried like a baby. Then the boss, Charley Weeghman, stuck his head in the door and issued a few choice profanities.

Such was the ending to a nearly perfect game. The game ended 1-0 but for nine innings each pitcher had no-hitters. It is remembered as one of the great pitching duels ever.

## CHAPTER 6

# 1918
# A Season Shortened By War

WORLD WAR I, nearly forgotten by the present generations in America, threw Major League Baseball a wicked curve. The government ordered MLB to finish its season by September and there would be no more baseball for the duration of the war. At the time it appeared the War could go on for many months or years.

This was the first "big war" to challenge America since the end of the Great American Civil War. The Spanish American War had reacquainted Americans with war and a few veterans of that foray could now be found on the professional baseball diamonds.

But this Great War, billed as the "war to end all wars", brought with it the draft. Able bodied men would be conscripted to service. It is said World War I actually began with the assassination of Franz Ferdinand, heir to the Austro-Hungarian throne, in Sarajevo on June 28, 1914. One by one nations aligned and before long, threats of war became actual combat. Russia, France and England and their lesser allies were soon united against Germany and Austria. The United States, under the guiding hand of President Woodrow Wilson, embraced neutrality until Germany declared unrestricted submarine warfare. This threatened American shipping commerce. The United States entered the war on the side of England, Russia and France on April 6, 1917.

A great horror accompanied this war. Reports of the use of deadly poisonous gas on the battlefield struck fear in the hearts of America. Almost simultaneously reports spread that professional baseball players would be exempt from the draft. America was outraged. To counter this, many baseball players enlisted and were trained on their practice fields. But in 1917 the baseball playing went on until the expiration of the season and the World Series played.

In 1918 it looked for a time that the baseball season in the Major Leagues would be cancelled. Finally a decision was reached that required the season to be completed earlier and the World Series played in early September. Many of the minor league teams simply cancelled their seasons as many good ball players had already donned military uniforms and were already serving in the European theatre.

One of the most notable casualties of the war was Captain Eddie Grant. Grant had already retired from baseball in 1915 and began practicing as a lawyer. He had graduated from Harvard in 1905. His major league career began at the very end of the 1905 season when he got a tryout and earned a temporary position with the Cleveland Indians. He was sent down to the minors in the 1906 season but came back a year later to play for the Philadelphia Athletics. He earned a good reputation as an infielder and a base stealer. He also played for the Cincinnati Reds and was traded to the New York Giants in 1913[31]. Grant was one of the first to volunteer following the outbreak of war. He was commissioned a Captain and assigned to the 77th Infantry Division. His unit was assigned to the bloody fighting in the Meuse-Argonne Forest. All of his commanding officers were wiped out in the fighting and he was put in charge of a unit trying to find a lost battalion of soldiers. During the four-day search an artillery shell exploded near him and killed him. Grant was buried in France. Grant was the first professional baseball player to die in World War I.[32]

Alex Burr, an outfielder for the 1914 New York Yankees, died in a plane crash in France in October 1918.[33] Robert Gustav "Bun" Troy also died in France in October 1918. Troy pitched for the 1912 Detroit Tigers.

Perhaps the most tragic impact caused by the war on Major League Baseball was to a group of players who went to war and were transferred to France. The group consisted of Ty Cobb, Christy Mathewson, Branch Rickey, George Sisler, Pete Alexander, Gabby Street, Hank Gowdy, and Clarence Mitchell.

"I saw Christy Mathewson doomed to die, Ty Cobb said of the disaster in his autobiography *My Life in Baseball:*"

The Germans introduced poisonous gas warfare in 1915 and killed thousands of their enemies. The ball players mentioned above were assigned to a U.S. Army facility in France which trained soldiers in the use of newly improved gas masks. While there was great improvement in the ability of

---

[31] http://en.wikipedia.org/wiki/Eddie_Grant_(baseball)
[32] http://en.wikipedia.org/wiki/Lost_Battalion_(World_War_I)
[33] http://www.baseball-reference.com/players/b/burra101.shtml

the masks to reduce deaths on the battlefield, the training suffered from short-sightedness. The men were trained using a very deadly chlorine gas.

On this particular day of training a signal to put on masks that deadly gas was about to be released was missed by several of the trainees, including the players. It was a lethal error. A period of chaos and panic ensued and many men who breathed the gas died. Others like Mathewson got a not-immediately-deadly whiff of gas.[34]

Two of the greatest players in baseball history came out traumatized and broken. Mathewson, the most winning pitcher in the National League and nicknamed "The Big Six", eventually developed tuberculosis—attributed to breathing the gas—and died before being inducted in the Baseball Hall of Fame. He did serve two years as a coach for the Giants, but missed much of both seasons as he was off getting medical treatment. He died in Lake Saranac, New York and is buried in Pleasanton, Pennsylvania. His hometown of Factoryville, Pennsylvania still celebrates the Saturday closest to his birthday (August 12, 1880) as a local holiday.[35]

Grover Cleveland "Pete" Alexander served as an artillery officer during the war. His minor league experiences were inauspicious. Playing for Galesburg, Illinois, of the Central Association in 1909, he tried to break up a double play and took the shortstop's relay directly in the head. Unconscious for two days, he awoke with double vision. Galesburg sent him to Indianapolis of the American Association, but, still disoriented, he broke three of the manager's ribs with his first pitch. Indianapolis sent him home and sold his contract to the Syracuse Chiefs of the International League over the winter. By spring, his vision had cleared and he won 29 for the Chiefs, including 15 shutouts.[36] From there his fame and record skyrocketed. By the end of the 1917 season Alexander had won 190 games for the Philly team. When he received a draft notice, the Philadelphia owner traded him to the Chicago Cubs.[37] John Skipper describes in his book *Wicked Curve* how two of the great pitchers in early baseball were destroyed by the war.

---

[34] My Life in Baseball: The True Story by Ty Cobb with Al Stump, originally published by Doubleday 1961, "Bison", pp.190-192

[35] http://en.wikipedia.org/wiki/Christy_Mathewson

[36] http://www.baseballlibrary.com/ballplayers/player.php?name=Grover_Cleveland_Alexander_1887

[37] http://en.wikipedia.org/wiki/Grover_Cleveland_Alexander

Alexander and Mathewson were the winningest pitchers in the National League at the time of their induction. Alexander returned to baseball unable to hear in his left ear due to serving in the artillery. His right ear had been hit with shrapnel and had to be amputated years later when the ear became cancerous. He also developed shoulder and bicep problems in his pitching arm.

The war probably also acerbated his *secret affliction*. Old Pete, as he was known to his contemporaries, suffered from epilepsy, a little understood disease at the time. He fought the problem by self medicating with alcohol. The seizures worsened after the war and so did Old Pete's drinking problem.

When the Phillies learned their 30-game winning pitcher was going to war, they traded him to the Chicago Cubs. What Chicago got back after the war was a badly damaged veteran who would have to battle pain, disease and personal demons the rest of his days. [38]

Problems or not, Alexander gave the Cubs nine great seasons racking up 128 wins against 87 losses. Yet dealing with his drinking took a toll. He was traded to the St. Louis Cardinals in 1926. The Cardinals won the World Series with Old Pete saving in the seventh and final game. He had won the second and sixth games himself. He was voted Most Valuable Player for the 1926 series. He won more than 200 games after returning from service in World War I.

We are not certain how Cy spent the war years. The rule of baseball was to serve in uniform or in a defense industry. Farms and railroads were both essential industries. Perhaps he served in one or both.

---

[38] John Skipper, *Wicked Curve, The Life and Troubled Times of Grover Cleveland Alexander*, McFarland & company 0786424125 or review http://www.goodreads.com/book/show/1541566.Wicked_Curve

# CHAPTER 7

# The Triple I League

WE LAST FOUND Cy playing ball in Fort Wayne, Indiana. In 1919 he resurfaces pitching for the Evansville Evas in Evansville Indiana. Evansville belonged to the Triple I League (Illinois, Indiana, Iowa). Evansville is just 50 miles from the place of Cy's birth. While the Evas were not exactly a star-stubbed team, they were a conglomeration of minor leaguers, many of whom, like Cy, would experience glimpses of glory. These men were riding the merry-go-round called professional baseball. Some were headed to the big leagues, and some were already back from their fickle date with destiny. Going or coming, they often answered to colorful nicknames that, like as not, said something about them. They included:

- **Al Bashang**: Playing left field for the Evas. Born in Cincinnati, he was a 1912 teammate of Ty Cobb in 1912 and played for the Brooklyn Robins in 1918. His baseball career stretching from 1910 to 1927 would include playing on more than 20 minor league teams.[39]
- **Stanley W. "Rabbit" Benton**, born in Cannel City, Kentucky in 1901. Rabbit who would play six games for the Philadelphia Phillies in 1922.[40]
- Edward **James "Irish" Conwell,** a Chicago boy, who went to bat once for the St. Louis Cardinals in 1911[41]
- **Charlie High**, right fielder, born in Ava, Illinois in December 1898, would not finish out the 1919 season with the Evansville Evas. He would be called up by the Philadelphia Athletics to play in 11 games and then play another 17 games the 1920 season. Injury may have been a reason for his release in 1920. He was batting .308 when released. The great Connie Mack was once asked why

---

[39] http://www.baseball-reference.com/minors/player.cgi?id=bashan001alb
[40] http://www.baseball-reference.com/players/b/bentora01.shtml
[41] http://www.baseball-reference.com/players/c/conweed01.shtml

his team was losing so many games replied: "Because I got High." Charlie went to the plate 35 times and had a batting average (BA) of .069. The next year he made up for it, batting .308. He was however sent back to the minors. [42]

- **Mike Kelley**, born November 1902 in St. Louis, pitched six innings of ball for the Phillies in 1923. He allowed nine hits, walked four batters and committed seven errors. He would only play four seasons of minor league ball.
- **Charles Elmer "Punch" Knoll**, born in Evansville in October 1881 and died there in February of 1960. Knoll had a successful year in 1905 when he played three positions for the Washington Senators/Nationals. The Nationals used him in the outfield in 63 games. He also filled in at catcher, and at first base in seven additional games. He batted in 79 games but sported a meager .213 BA.[43]
- **Joseph Patrick "Shags" Horan**, born September 6, 1895, would play outfield for the 1924 New York Yankees. He would watch Babe Ruth launch 46 home runs.[44]
- The real Mister Big League of the Evas of 1919 was **Doug "Buzz" McWeeny**. McWeeny, born in Chicago in August 1896, was destined to start his major league career with the "reborn" Chicago White Sox in 1921. He repeated in 1922. He missed the 1923 season and then returned in 1924. He also missed the 1925 season. In 1926 through 1929 he pitched for the Brooklyn Robins. His final game was June 17, 1930. His career concluded with 948 innings pitched and 116 games started. McWeeny was a regular on the leader boards of the National League in 1926 through 1929. He won 37 games and lost 57 but his value was in relieving. He saved 116 games.[45]

Unfortunately we don't know much about the 1919 season. The records have not survived. What we can add is the fact that the team averaged 25.2 years of age and that the coach was an apparently colorful baseballer by the name of **Johnny Nee**. Nee apparently never made it to the majors. Nee had been the player/manager for the Dayton Veterans in 1917. (Cy

---

[42] http://www.baseball-reference.com/players/h/highch01.shtml
[43] http://www.baseball-reference.com/players/k/knollpu01.shtml
[44] http://www.baseball-reference.com/players/h/horansh01.shtml
[45] http://www.baseball-reference.com/players/m/mcweedo01.shtml

and the Fort Wayne Chiefs played the veterans in the last season before the intervention of World War I.)

Nee, born Jan 18, 1890 in Thayer, Mo, began his baseball career as a catcher for the Springfield/Webb City, Missouri Midgets. This was Class C ball. He continued for the Midgets until going to play for the St. Paul, Minnesota Saints. Here he was one of the few players who did not go onto play major league ball.

Johnny Nee played and coached on a variety of teams in a career that lasted until 1926. He was active in the Central League, the Illinois-Indiana-Iowa League, the Texas League, Western League and the Virginia League. Nee died in St. Petersburg, Florida in 1957; his death preceded Cy's passing by only three months.

It seems that while playing for Eva's that Cy encountered his third Hall of Famer (although the HOF had not yet been conceived). The Terre Haute Browns were using a 43-year old pitcher who had established quite a reputation in the majors. His name was Mordecai "Three Fingered" Brown. A native Hoosier, having been born in Nyesville, Indiana in 1876, Brown won more than 60 percent of the games he pitched in Major League Baseball. He started for the Cardinals in 1903 having been purchased from Omaha in the Western League and pitched 26 games. He started 24 and won only nine of them. In 1904 he moved to the Chicago Cubs where he would stay until signed with the Federal League in 1914. After the Federal League folded he went back to the Cubs for two more seasons. He left the majors in 1916 and went back to the minors. He played in the American Association for Columbus and Indianapolis before making a "hometown" season for Terre Haute.

His nickname came from the fact that at age seven he lost the end of an index finger and mangled his little finger on the right hand in a corn sheller. His hand deformities enabled him to throw an oddly breaking curveball.[46]

## *Elsewhere in baseball in 1919.*

The World Series scandal of 1919 rattled America and shook faith in the game to the point of near ruination. The focal team in the scandal was the Chicago White Sox and sometimes "the Black Sox" to commemorate

---

[46] Lawrence Ritter and Donald Honig, *The 100 Greatest Baseball Players of All Time,* Crown Publishers, Inc., New York pp 76

the team's fall into infamy. The first player to report involvement was none other than "Shoeless Joe" Jackson, one of the greatest hitters the game has ever known. His involvement has never quite been totally explained but several of his teammates later came forward to say he had not attended meetings on the sinister plot. Yet he testified to have taken $5,000 from Lefty Williams, another White Sox Pitcher who was deeply involved in "the fix".

Some say one of the great villians was none other than White Sox owner Charles Comiskey who had founded the team as the Chicago White Stockings in 1900. They shortened the name to the White Sox in 1902. The team was immediately successful. In 1910 Comiskey built a palatial stadium which he named for himself. His flair for pomp and grandeur earned him the nickname "The Old Roman." His players found him to be more like "Old Scrooge."

In 1903 the owners of the National and American Leagues had agreed to a post meeting series between the two leagues which would be called "The World Series." That too was an extreme success and quickly became a major event for Americans. By 1919. baseball team owners were surprised how much interest there was in baseball so soon after the conclusion of the war. In order to make more gate money, they increased the world series from a best of seven games to a best of nine.

If Comiskey was a wonderful success as a businessman, he was a scalawag and tyrant as an employer. He was a notorious cheapskate and missed no opportunity to pay low wages. Even worse he often pitted the players against each other.

One year Comiskey promised his players a big bonus if they won the pennant. When they were league champions, he plied them not with money but cheap champagne. Comiskey charged his players for laundering their uniforms. In rebellion, the players wore the same, increasingly dirty, uniforms for weeks. Comiskey took their uniforms from their lockers and fined them for their appearance.

One of his dirtiest "tricks" fell upon pitcher Eddie Cicotte. Comiskey promised him a $10,000 bonus if he won 30 games. When Cicotte won his 29th game Comiskey benched him and told him he needed rest, for the pennant games. Cicotte never got his win and Comiskey never paid him the bonus.[47] What is most surprising about Comiskey is that he was an ex-player. He started as a $50-per-month pitcher for the Dubuque, Iowa

---

[47] http://www.chicagohs.org/history/blacksox/blk3.html

Rabbits. When his arm gave out, he moved to first base and proved to be a great defensive tactician. He played six years for the team, five of them as player/ manager. He taught his players to position themselves on the field according to where batters had previously hit. He was industrious and is said to have made a lot of money selling candy and newspapers to passengers on the Illinois Central Railroad.

Comiskey implemented his own pay scales at the White Sox. While all his players were underpaid, some were more badly paid than others. His team divided itself into jealous factions.[48] One faction consisted of educated, sophisticated players who had negotiated salaries up to $15,000 per year. The other players were knowledgable only in baseball. There incomes ranged in the vicinity of $6,000 per year. There was constant warfare between the groups. The "haves" were led by second baseman Eddie Collins. The "have nots" were led by First Baseman Chick Gandil.

Gamblers frequented all major league ball parks long before this scandal broke. They were always looking to make a bet and needed inside information and some players could be bribed. One such frequenter was Joseph Sullivan. Gandil, on the brink of retirement, apparently approached Sullivan and told him for a payment of $100,000 he could hire enough White Sox players to throw the 1919 World Series. Gandil first recruited the pitchers Eddie Ciotti and Lefty Williams who had won 52 games between them that season. The other players eventually fingered were: Shoeless Joe" Jackson, infielders Buck Weaver, Arnold Fred McMullin, and Charles "Swede" Risberg; and outfielder Oscar "Happy" Felsch.

The aftermath was best summarized by Traci Patterson, on a website summary of the legal proceedings:

> "Following the World Series of 1919 Comiskey offered a reward of $20,000 to anyone who could provide information about the rumored fix. He placed an ad in newspapers across the country. Several people came forward to provide information, including a letter received from Joe Jackson written by his wife, but the reward was never paid. "Comiskey was called as a witness at the trial of the eight White Sox players. He revealed that he had heard possible rumors of the fix during the series.

---

[48] http://www.law.umkc.edu/faculty/projects/ftrials/blacksox/comiskeybio.html

Comiskey was also questioned about the finances of the White Sox team during the years surrounding the scandal. He could not remember exact figures. The defense hit a nerve with Comiskey when they questioned him about possible contract jumping when he was a baseball player. He became irate and was dismissed from the stand. The White Sox players were represented at trial by some of the most expensive lawyers in the area. However, none of the players had enough money to afford their services. Comiskey, it turned out, paid the attorney fees.

"Judge Kennesaw Mountain Landis banned the eight former White Sox players from playing professional baseball for life after their acquittal. Comiskey publicly proclaimed his full support for Landis's decision. Yet, this destroyed his top ranked baseball team and their dominance of the league soon ended.

"Charles Comiskey had two nicknames in his lifetime. Some called him "Old Roman" because of his physical makeup and personal traits. He was known by his friends simply as "Commy." Comiskey died in 1931 at the age of 72 in his Wisconsin summer home."—Traci Patterson, 3L/ University of Missouri-Kansas City School of Law [49]

"Shoeless Joe" Jackson was so nicknamed because when a minor league manager would not get him a pair of better fitting shoes, he played barefoot. He had a BA of .408 in 1911. It is the sixth highest batting average for a single season since 1900. He played baseball in five seasons before being banned from baseball forever by Commissioner Judge Landis. His involvement in the scandal did not prevent him from reaching status as a legend but it kept him out of the Hall of Fame.

## INDIANA'S BASEBALL PRODIGY

Cy's involvement in Evansville baseball was not a bad thing. One local boy had already proven you could get to the majors from Evansville. In 1912 Edd J. Roush reported to Coach Fred Barton hoping to play for the Evansville, Indiana team. He was 19 years old. He was born May 8, 1893 in

---

[49] http://www.law.umkc.edu/faculty/projects/ftrials/blacksox/comiskeybio.html

nearby Oakland City, Indiana. The kid was a baseball prodigy and probably the only Hall of Famer to launch his career from the "Kitty" League. The official name of the league was the Kentucky-Illinois-Tennessee League and it had a "D" Classification. This was not a league where one would expect greatness to be found. Only one other player on the 1912 team would reach the pros. Edd Rousch was a special young man.

In 1913 Roush made his major league career debut for the Chicago White Sox. Like Cy, he would meet initial disappointment. He would play in nine games, bat ten times but only get a single hit. The Sox would release him and he would come back to play for the Evansville River Rats which was a Class B team playing in the Central League. Later he would swing out to Lincoln Nebraska to play 10 games for the Lincoln Railsplitters. The Railsplitters played in the Class A Western League. It was a "big town" league. Opponents included the Denver Bears, the Des Moines Boosters, as well as teams from Omaha, Sioux City, Topeka, Wichita and St. Joseph, Missouri.

In 1914 Rousch was invited to play in the newly formed Federal League, which was considered a Major League. He hit an astounding .325 for the Indianapolis Hoosiers while playing outfield. The following year he found himself on the roster of the Newark Peppers in the same league and averaged .298 in 145 games. He had established his prowess as a hitter.

Following the collapse of the Federal League he went to the Cincinnati Reds of the National League and hit .287 in 69 games. Later that year he went to the New York Giants. Roush would divide the rest of his career between these two teams. He retired as a Red September 27, 1931 after playing 1,967 major league games and went to the plate 5,965 times. He racked up 2,376 hits and scored 1,099 times. His lifetime batting average was .323. Roush was elected to the Hall of Fame in 1962. He died in Bradenton Florida March 21, 1988[50]

---

[50] http://www.baseball-reference.com/players/r/roushed01.shtml

# CHAPTER 8

# Off To Nashville In A New Era

## 1921

WHILE CY WAS playing ball in Evansville, the world turned. In fact there came three changes in a short period of which truly changed baseball.

**Change#1: A Livelier Baseball**

When American soldiers were sent to fight they needed many supplies. Material shortages of many commodities developed. One of the first items to be in short supply was the high quality yarn needed to make baseballs. Baseball makers responded by selecting a lower quality yard but it was found the substitute yarn wound much more loosely than the yarn originally used. Manufacturers such as A.G. Spalding responded by increasing the tightness of the wind. (The yarn is wound by machines.) The end result was a baseball much more lively than the original.

Almost like a Chinese dynasty, baseball historians now divide the sport into specific eras. Two of the first periods were "The Dead Ball" era (before 1920). The time since is known as "The Live Ball Era." The second era is said to favor the batters, where the first era favored the pitchers.[51] The ball would be livened one more time during the depression years.

We have alluded to the stinginess of Major League Baseball and most of its owners. One of the strangest cost saving measures was their reluctance to replace a baseball. Today when we watch games, the umpire looks at the baseball and if it has a scuff or smudge, out it goes and a brand new one comes into the game. Not so in the old days. The ball was in the game until someone knocked it into the stands or became so deformed the pitcher couldn't control it. Fans were even expected to throw back the foul balls. Kids were given free passes if they returned balls knocked out of the ballpark.

---

[51] http://www.thedeadballera.com/mayschapman.html

## Change #2: End of the Spitball

Spit balls were legal until this year when Major League Baseball owners agreed to phase it out. Yet, in deference to some of the "name" pitchers who used the "spitter", and had for years, it was decided that the pitch would be phased out. Seventeen players were granted permission to keep using it. They were:

1. The first "spitter" to leave the game was **Ray Fisher**, a native Vermonter, who retired from Major League Ball in 1920. His story is filled with ups and downs, much of it caused by team owners' unbridled power. Fisher was banned for life for having decided to coach the University of Michigan baseball team after signing a contract to play for Cincinnati. He had been placed on waivers by the Yankees after completing his hitch in the Army. The Reds wanted to pay him $3,100 less than $6,600 the New York Highlanders (Yankees) had paid him. Ty Cobb said he was one of the top twelve pitchers ever in the American League. He was very successful after eventually taking the coaching position at Michigan. He guided Michigan for 38 seasons and won 14 Big Ten Championships and the 1953 College World Series Championship. His ban from professional baseball was overturned; he was the first player to ever earn that honor.[52]
2. **Yancey Wyatt "Doc" Ayers** from Snake Creek, Virginia. He retired at season's end 1921. He played for the Nationals for many years and once relieved Babe Ruth who was pitching for the Boston Red Sox. Ruth walked the first batter and then got thrown out of the game for arguing with the umpire. Ayres retired 26 consecutive batters and earned a no-hitter. His manager removed him in the ninth inning to put in a pinch hitter.[53]
3. **Ray Caldwell,** who, while pitching for the Cleveland Indians against the Philadelphia. Athletics in 1919, was struck by lightning. Although knocked unconscious, he refused to leave the game and got up and finished the pitching job.[54]
4. **Phil Douglas,** a great pitcher with a drinking problem. He quarreled with Giants owner John McGraw in the 1922 season and

---

[52] http://en.wikipedia.org/wiki/Ray_Fisher
[53] http://en.wikipedia.org/wiki/Doc_Ayers
[54] http://en.wikipedia.org/wiki/Ray_Caldwell

McGraw fined him $100. He won two games in the 1921 World Series and helped the Giants cinch the series. After being fined he wrote a letter to a member of the St. Louis Cardinals saying if he had some" inducement" he would quit the Giants. When baseball commission Kennesaw Landis found out about the letter he banned Douglas from baseball for life.[55]

Four more "grandfathered" spitballers retired in 1925. They were

5. **Marvin "Mardo" Goodwin**,[56]
6. **Allen "Rubberarm" Russell**[57],
7. **Dana Fillingim**[58] and
8. **Dutch Leonard**[59].

Leonard is most known of the four. His feud with Ty Cobb as player and manager are well recorded. In 1914 he had an ERA of .96, a modern era record. Rubberarm Russell was a teammate of Cy in Washington.

9. **Allen Sothoron,** retired in 1926, pitched 11 seasons in the majors. His teams were the St. Louis Browns, Boston Red Sox, Cleveland Indians and St. Louis Cardinals. He was assistant manager of the Cardinals until replaced by a young upstart by the name of Rogers Hornsby.[60]
10. **Richard Rudolph** retired in 1927. He pitched for the Boston Braves and the New York Giants.[61]
11. **Urban** (not a nickname) **Shocker** was a standout pitcher of the era. He once pitched 54 consecutive scoreless innings for the New York Yankees. He also played for the St. Louis Browns (in a bad trade engineered by Miller Huggins) for a short time before going back to the Yankees.[62] Shocker left Major League Baseball in 1928.

---

55 http://www.baseball-reference.com/players/r/rudoldi01.shtml
56 http://en.wikipedia.org/wiki/Marv_Goodwin
57 http://en.wikipedia.org/wiki/Allen_Russell_(baseball)
58 http://en.wikipedia.org/wiki/Dana_Fillingim
59 http://en.wikipedia.org/wiki/Dutch_Leonard_(left-handed_pitcher)
60 http://en.wikipedia.org/wiki/Allen_Sothoron
61 http://en.wikipedia.org/wiki/Dick_Rudolph
62 http://en.wikipedia.org/wiki/Urban_Shocker

12. **Stan Covelski** also left baseball in 1928. His teams included Philadelphia, Cleveland, Washington and New York.[63]
13. **William Leopold "Bill" Doak** quit as a player in 1929. Doak, a native of Pittsburgh, made his mark for the St. Louis Cardinals but also played a short time for the Brooklyn Robins. Although he did not always have a strong team, he always pitched well and is one of the great St. Louis pitchers of all times. His 32 shutouts are second only to Hall of Famer Bob Gibson.[64]

The last of the grandfathered "spitters" bowed out in the 1930's.

14. **Clarence Mitchell,** who played for six major league teams, retired in 1932.
15. **Jack Quinn,** who has a variety of "oldest to do" awards didn't leave major league baseball until he was 50 years old. He played for eight teams in three leagues (American, National and Federal). He was born in Slovakia and immigrated to America as an infant. He retired in 1933.[65]
16. **Urban Clarence "Red" Faber** was the last legal spitballer in the American League. He left baseball in 1933. He played 19 years for the Chicago White Sox. He was ill and did not play during the scandalous 1919 World Series. It was said that if he had been healthy, the White Sox fix would never have been possible. He had suffered from a sore arm and flu in the 1919 influenza epidemic.[66]
17. **Burleigh Grimes** was the last major leaguer to throw a spitball legally. He retired in 1934. Known to his teammates as "Ol' Stubblebeard." He played for Pittsburgh, the Brooklyn Dodgers, the New York Giants, the Boston Braves, the St. Louis Cardinals and the Chicago Cubs. It took thirteen seasons to eliminate the spitball.

Cy Warmoth would play with and against several of these favored pitchers.

---

[63] http://en.wikipedia.org/wiki/Stan_Coveleski
[64] http://en.wikipedia.org/wiki/Bill_Doak
[65] http://en.wikipedia.org/wiki/Jack_Quinn_(baseball)
[66] http://en.wikipedia.org/wiki/Red_Faber

## Change #3 The Mays-Chapman Incident

The third thing to change baseball is referred to as the Mays-Chapman Incident.

Ray Chapman, star shortstop-second baseman and a .300 hitter for the Cleveland Indians was batting against Carl Mays of the New York Yankees. Chapman, a 29-year old Kentuckian, was playing his 1,051st game for the Indians. Chapman, who joined the team in 1912, when it was called the Cleveland Naps, was enjoying his ninth season.[67]

Carl Mays was a 5-11 195 pound right-handed pitcher looking for his 100th career win. The story is one of the most written about stories in baseball but I think it was best told on the deadballera.com website:

> Chapman used a crouching stance when batting. Witnesses said he crowded the plate more than normal against Mays that day because he had never hit well when Mays was pitching. On his first trip to the plate he hit a sacrifice bunt. The second time up he crowded the plate. Mays pitched him twice throwing Chapman a ball and a strike. The third pitch went high and inside. Chapman never ducked and the ball hit him in the left side of the head just above the ear. Chapman made no effort to duck the pitch. The impact was so hard the ball rolled towards the pitchers mound. Mays thought the ball had hit Chapman's bat. He scooped up the ball and threw it to first base to make the out. Chapman got up and tried to get to first base but collapsed after two steps. They rushed him to the clubhouse and he seemed to be coming around.
>
> "I'm all right, tell Mays not to worry," he told those attending him. He was taken to St. Lawrence Hospital in Manhattan. "Chappy's" condition continued to deteriorate at the hospital and doctors decided to operate. The operation began shortly after midnight. The doctor removed a 3.-1/2 inch piece of bone on the left side of his skull. It was also found he had damage to both sides of the brain and severe clotting. Chapman died at 4:40 a.m.[68]

There were many ramifications to the incident. Many thought the "beaning" was intentional and there were numerous attempts to get Mays banned from baseball. He was finally cleared after an investigation by a

---

[67] http://www.baseball-reference.com/players/
[68] http://www.thedeadballera.com/mayschapman.html

private investigation firm. The tragedy grew. Chapman's wife remarried and moved to California but she continued to be depressed. She committed suicide in 1926. Her daughter with whom she was pregnant at the time of Mays death died of measles two years later.

Mays wife also died, her death was attributed to "complications of an eye infection." In the era of yellow journalism, Mays was berated by many major league ballplayers as well as the press. He was accused of having thrown ball games and lost favor with his teammates and with his coach Miller Huggins (The same coach Cy had tried out for in the St. Louis Cardinals team in 1916.) Mays struggled but stayed in major league baseball. He was traded to Cincinnati and lastly to the New York Giants. He won another 101 games before he retired from the New York Giants. He worked as a baseball scout for another 20 years. He insisted until his death that he had throw inside but was not trying to hit Chapman.

Chapman's death demonstrated how much force a hurled baseball could do to the human anatomy. Players began sneaking padding into their ball caps. Major League Baseball would begin to look more seriously at protective equipment. These players had the scantiest of equipment. Catchers and umpires had minimal padding. Players had un-webbed gloves not much better than a modern leather work glove. [69]

Incidentally, the 1952 Pittsburg Pirates were the first to wear safety helmets. Pirate players were required to keep them on even when fielding. It is interesting to note that the ear flap was designed for Little Leaguers, but Major League Baseball liked the innovation and adopted it for professional players.[70]

Baseball shin guards made their debut in 1907 when New York Giants Roger Bresnahan catcher wore them on opening day. They saved his legs when a sharp foul ball banged them during the game. They were soon standard equipment.

There was one other piece of equipment that would affect Cy Warmoth's career: spikes on baseball shoes. In the year following his tour in Nashville, he would be involved in an incident that would mar his baseball career.

While all these incidents and rule changes were swirling around baseball, Cy Warmoth was growing better as a baseball pitcher.

---

[69] http://www.thedeadballera.com/aftermath.html
[70] http://library.thinkquest.org/J002934/Equipment.html

# Things We Know About Cy Warmoth

Let's stop to recap some of the things we know about Cy Warmoth in the year he was sent to "the high minors" in Nashville.

First of all he was 28 years old. In modern day professional baseball it would be said that he was getting old. That was not the case in the start of the lively ball era. We have already discussed how Jack Quinn pitched until age 50. Owners had different expectations of pitchers in this period.

What qualities did a good pitcher possess? Here are some things baseball managers were looking for:

1. <u>Speed:</u> While they did not have radar to measure pitching speeds, they liked a pitcher who could throw hard. Pitchers like Walter Johnson fired the ball so hard it almost disappeared.
2. <u>Control:</u> The ability to put the ball over the plate was essential. Batters liked to crowd the plate so it was often necessary to pitch inside without hitting the batter.
3. <u>Spin:</u> An ideal pitcher would not only have had the aforementioned qualities, but also a full array of specialty pitches. He would need to know a variety of ways to spin the ball so it would curve, break, rise or dip.
4. <u>Knowledge of Batters</u>: A pitcher needed to have mental notes of the other batters he faced. It was necessary to study stance, how the bat was held and even the bat he was using. Batters used their own bats in this period. Some were even hand carved. Ty Cobb used to have his bats made by The Louisville Slugger Company. Then he would spend countless hours "boning" his bat. He actually used a large hollowed out thigh bone of a steer. He also soaked the bats with tobacco juice or neet's foot oil. He preferred his bats to be made from ash lumber harvested in Kentucky or Tennessee.
5. <u>Durability</u>: A good pitcher had to be able to pitch a full game and extra innings if required. The great Negro pitcher Satchel Paige pitched several complete double headers in the Negro leagues. One can imagine the comments pitchers of that era would make about modern pitchers. It would be interesting to know how Cy would react to the news that the Washington Nationals would sign a young hard-throwing right hander for $15.1 million and then assign him to the Harrisburg, Pennsylvania Nationals for development. We

have uncovered no financial records for Cy, but it is unlikely he ever made more than $4,000-$5,000 at the height of his career.
6. <u>Reliability.</u> Pitchers had to be dependable and ready to pitch any anytime. Just because you pitched a dozen innings the day before did not mean that you would be exempt from pitching in today's game.
7. <u>Sobriety.</u> Owners and managers did not want their players, especially their pitchers, getting drunk and partaking in bar room brawls.
8. <u>Healthy and able to nurse their own injuries</u>. There were no fancy whirlpools and few on duty physicians.

What we know of Cy makes us think he was reliable and steadfast. He had an additional attribute. Cy was left handed. Some of the best batters in the business, had difficulty hitting southpaws. His years on a tough minor league route had taught him a lot. He had played with enough former major leaguers to learn the subtle tricks of the trade. He is not making a lot of money. He probably earned between $50 and $100 per month. To still be out there and still be trying he must have had great desire and a love for the game.

When Cy reported to Nashville one of the first things he would have noticed is that the Nashville pitching staff was loaded with talent. He would work with another left hander who destined to make the big time. **Red Lucas** was just two years away from beginning 15 seasons in the majors. He would spend one season with the New York Giants, another year with the Boston Braves. He would then play eight seasons for Cincinnati and his last five years with the Pittsburgh Pirates. He would frequent the leader boards and get three nominations to the Baseball Hall of Fame. Unfortunately he was not selected.[71]

**George Washington Payne** was also on the pitching staff. He had already been called up and sent back down. He pitched two games for the Chicago White Sox in 1920, winning one and losing one. He is 31 years old.[72]

Thirty-eight year old **Hub Perdue** had also been up and sent back down. He played four years for the Boston Braves. When he was called up

---

[71] http://www.baseball-reference.com/minors/player.cgi?id=lucas-001cha
[72] http://www.baseball-reference.com/minors/player.cgi?id=payne-001geo

in 1911 the team was called the Boston Rustlers. He won 51 games and lost 64. He had been a teammate of Cy Young at Boston.[73]

Other major leaguers on the 1921 Nashville Team were:

**Hugh Bradley**, an old timer at 38 years of age, spent five seasons up top. His teams included Boston and three Federal League teams: Pittsburgh Rebels, the Brooklyn Tip Tops and the Newark Peppers.[74]

**Bubber Jonnard** caught for the White Sox in 1920 but was released. The trip to Nashville is one of several minor league interludes for Jonnard. He would catch for the pirates in 1922, the Phillies in 1926 and 1927, the Cardinals in 1929 and then after several years catch once more for the Phillies in 1935.[75] (Cy encounters the Jonnard name several times in his career.)

**Bill Stellbauer, 27,** played in the outfield for the Philadelphia Athletics. He played 25 games. [76]

**Tony Tonneman,** 39, appeared in two games for the Red Sox in 1911.[77]

The Nashville Volunteers played at home in Sulphur Springs Bottom Athletic Park in Nashville. Fans called it Old Sulfur Dell. In 1922 Cy and his team would have played in front of the original wooden grandstand. It was originally a field with a natural sulfur spring and social Nashville baseball clubs were playing organized here within a few years of the end of the Civil War. The park is said to have been in use for organized baseball clubs from 1870 until 1969. It is one of the most written about minor league parks in America. There is an entire webpage dedicated to it. (http://www.sulphurdell.com/Photos_.htm). The original ballpark is often mentioned in the memoirs of baseball players Many Major League ball clubs took spring training and played exhibition games here. The original grandstand "stadium" was torn down in 1926-1927. The concrete and steel stadium that replaced it is even more famous. The baseball field had an outfield with an uphill slope.

The Nashville team belonged to the prestigious Southern Association League and the league, as previously stated, had a reputation of finding

---

[73] http://www.baseball-reference.com/minors/player.cgi?id=perdue001her
[74] http://www.baseball-reference.com/minors/player.cgi?id=bradle001hug
[75] http://www.baseball-reference.com/players/j/jonnabu01.shtml
[76] http://www.baseball-reference.com/players/s/stellbi02.shtml
[77] http://www.baseball-reference.com/players/t/tonneto01.shtml

great talent which major league owners could raid at reasonable prices. Players coming into the Southern Association were prospects to move up. The men coming back to the minors were amiable, name-dropping braggarts, anxious to share their limelight experience. They were usually better ball players for their efforts and not afraid to show a younger man a few tricks.

Coming back from the big show made a man appreciate the quieter side of baseball. The owners and managers were more practical. Most had a realistic view of life and would talk to a man before they cast him into a fire. If you did a good job, played hard and kept the tickets, beer and popcorn selling, you had a good life.

The American Association of 1920 consisted of the following teams and with them is a list of major league players who would go or had returned (coming back or going) to the big show.

1. **Atlanta Crackers: Phil Bedgood**, pitched for the Indians in 1922-23 (going)[78]; **Fred Graf,** played third base for St. Louis Browns in 1913. (coming)[79]; **Dick Kaufmann,** played first base for the St. Louis Browns in 1914-1915 (coming)[80]; **Cliff Markle**, pitched for New York Yankees in 1915-1916 and Cincinnati Red Legs in 1921-1922 and went back to the Yankees Cincinnati in 1921 and 1922 and the Yankees in 1924. (coming and going) Note: Markle pitched a total of 29 games in the majors. His record was 12-17[81]; **Sam Mayer,** pitcher and first baseman for Yankees in 1915, (coming)[82]; **Buddy Napier,** pitched 11 games in the majors over a five year period for the Browns, Cubs and Red Legs (coming and going)[83]; **Tiny Osborne**, pitched four seasons in the majors for the Brooklyn Robins and Chicago Cubs and had a 32-40 record (going)[84]; **Bill Rariden**, spent 12 seasons in the majors from 1909-1920, played for Boston through three name changes (Doves, Rustlers and Braves), Hoosiers, Newark Peppers, Giants and Red

---

[78] http://www.baseball-reference.com/players/b/bedgoph01.shtml
[79] http://www.baseball-reference.com/players/g/grafffr01.shtml
[80] http://www.baseball-reference.com/players/k/kauffdi01.shtml
[81] http://www.baseball-reference.com/minors/player.cgi?id=markle001cli
[82] http://www.baseball-reference.com/players/m/mayersa01.shtml
[83] http://www.baseball-reference.com/players/n/napiebu01.shtml
[84] http://www.baseball-reference.com/players/o/osborti01.shtml

Legs, listed on leader boards in his early years (coming)[85]; **Boss Schmidt**, played for Detroit Tigers from 1906-1911 and played in 447 games and helped them win three pennants and lose three world series, (Note: He is mentioned in Ty Cobb's book as the antagonist on the Detroit Team who broke Cobb's baseball bats and nose, but later became a friend.)[86]; **Fred Smith,** second/third baseman/shortstop 1913-1917. He played for the Boston Braves and Cardinals and also three teams in the Federal Leagues. He played in 438 games in the majors. He was on the Leader Boards in the Federal League (coming)[87] **Al Wingo**, played on the 1919 Philadelphia Athletics, and played five seasons for Detroit. He went to the plate over 1500 times in the majors. (going)[88]

2. <u>Birmingham Barrons:</u> **Spoke Emery,** outfielder, played five games for Philadelphia in 1924 (going)[89]; **Johnny Gooch,** catcher, would leave before this season is over to join the Pittsburgh Pirates and stay in the majors for eleven seasons. He would play three games in the 1925 World Series against the Washington Nationals. They won the world series 4-3 in seven games. He also played three games in the 1927 series which was swept by the Yankees in four games (going).[90] **Phil Morrison** would be called up to pitch one game for the Pittsburgh Pirates. He would return to Birmingham the following season (going)[91]; **Stuffy Stewart**, 2nd-3rd baseman and outfielder was a member of the St. Louis Cardinals team in 1916-1917. He also played for the Pirates, Brooklyn Robins, and Washington Nationals. He would play in 176 games and appear at the plate 289 times. (coming/going)[92]; **Tommy Taylor**, would only play one season in the majors, but it would be a special one. He would join the Washington Nationals in a year when they would win their first world series. He would play second base, third base and outfield in three different games. He would go to

---

[85] http://www.baseball-reference.com/players/r/raridbi01.shtml
[86] http://www.baseball-reference.com/players/s/schmibo01.shtml
[87] http://www.baseball-reference.com/players/s/smithfr05.shtml
[88] http://www.baseball-reference.com/players/w/wingoal01.shtml
[89] http://www.baseball-reference.com/players/e/emerysp01.shtml
[90] http://www.baseball-reference.com/players/g/goochjo01.shtml
[91] http://www.baseball-reference.com/minors/player.cgi?id=morris002phi
[92] http://www.baseball-reference.com/players/s/stewast01.shtml

the plate twice and strike out twice (going).⁹³ **Pie Traynor, Hall of Fame third baseman,** got his tryout with the Pirates in 1920. He played 17 games in 1920 and was returned to Birmingham. Late in 1921 he would be called back to the Pirates and play for seven more games. He would stay with the Pirates until 1937. He played in 1,941 regular season games and bat 8,293 times. His lifetime batting average was .320. He played in the 1925 and 1927 World Series. He was selected to the Hall of Fame in 1948. He was outstanding in the so-called "mud-mired series game of 1927. (going) ⁹⁴; **Rip Wheeler**, appeared in the major leagues four years. He pitched a total of four innings in two games for the Pirates in the seasons of 1921 and 1922. In 1923 he was called up by the Chicago Cubs. He pitched 24 innings in that season, and 125.1 innings in 1924. He won four games and lost eight in his short career (going).⁹⁵; **Earl Whitehill**, pitcher, got his call up in 1923. He won 285 major league games most of them for Detroit, the team that called him up. He also pitched for the Nationals in 1933 through 1936, two years for Cleveland Indians and one season for the Cubs. He was nominated for the Hall of Fame four times but not elected.⁹⁶(going); **"Jughandle" Johnny Morrison**, pitched seven innings for the Pirates in 1920 in 1922 he would be called back. He would go on to win a total of 103 major league games while losing 80. The last two years he pitched for Brooklyn. He pitched in three games in the Pirates 1925 series. He started the seventh game (the famous mud bog game) but was pinched out in the fourth inning. He finished out his career pitching for Atlanta in the Southern Association League in 1931 and 1932. (Going).

3. <u>**Chattanooga Lookouts**</u>**: Dan Boone** had already had a look by Philadelphia in 1919. In 1920 he pitched a few innings for Detroit. He would get similar chances from Cleveland in 1922 and 1923. His major league record would be eight wins and 13 losses (going)⁹⁷; **Fred "Fritz" Bratschi** would get his call from the majors this season. He would play outfield 16 games for the rebuilding

---

93  http://www.baseball-reference.com/players/t/tayloto01.shtml
94  http://www.baseball-reference.com/players/t/traynpi01.shtml
95  http://www.baseball-reference.com/players/w/wheelri01.shtml
96  http://www.baseball-reference.com/players/w/whiteea01.shtml
97  http://www.baseball-reference.com/players/b/booneda01.shtml

Chicago White Sox. He would go back to the minors for several years and then go to play for the White Sox again in 1926-27. He had a .269 batting average in the majors. [98] (going); **Harvey "Gink" Hendrick** was one of the best players Chattanooga would send forward to the majors. He appeared in the 1923 World Series with the Yankees. He played first and third bases and outfield. He spent 1923 and 1924 with the New York Yankees, 1925 with the Cleveland Indians, 1927-1920 with the Brooklyn Robins; he split 1931 between the Brooklyn Robins and the Cincinnati Red Legs, 1932 he split between the Cincinnati Red Legs and the Cardinals. In 1933 he was traded to Chicago Cubs and in 1934 he went to the Philadelphia Phillies He had a .293 batting average for his 11 seasons of major league service (going)[99]; **Shags Horan** would get his call up in 1924. He would play outfield for the New York Yankees. He did not get to play in the famed World Series game against the Washington Nationals. (going)[100]; **Ed McDonald** played third base for Boston. He played in 1911 for the Rustlers and 1912 for the Braves. He was on the roster for the Chicago Cubs in 1913. (coming)[101]; Pitcher **Bob Vines** would get his call up from the St. Louis Cardinals in 1924 and the Philadelphia Phillies in 1925 (going). He only pitched 14.2 innings in both seasons. (going)[102]; Pitcher **Ted Wingfield** would pitch one inning for the Nationals in 1923 and another seven in 1924. In 1925 the Boston Red Sox would extend him another opportunity and a handful of appearances. But in 1926 the Red Sox would use him extensively, pitching in 119 innings in 20 games. In 1927 the Boston Red Sox would use him in another 22 games. His major league pitching record would be 24-44. He would spend three years in the minors before retiring.[103] (going).

4. **The Little Rock Travelers: Travis Jackson,** born in Waldo, Arkansas, was destined to be one of great major leaguers of all times and a member of **The Baseball Hall of Fame.** He would

---

[98] http://www.baseball-reference.com/players/b/bratsfr01.shtml
[99] http://www.baseball-reference.com/players/h/hendrha01.shtml
[100] http://www.baseball-reference.com/players/h/horansh01.shtml
[101] http://www.baseball-reference.com/players/m/mcdoned02.shtml
[102] http://www.baseball-reference.com/players/v/vinesbo01.shtml
[103] http://www.baseball-reference.com/players/w/wingfte01.shtml

get his call up in 1922 and remain with the same team, the New York Giants for 15 seasons. He would appear in the World Series four times. A short stop and third baseman, he was also selected to the 1934 All Star game. He played seven games in the 1924 series against the Washington Nationals which is considered one of the best World Series in baseball. He batted more than 6,000 times and maintained an impressive .291 batting average. He was elected to the **Hall of Fame** in 1982.[104] (going).; Pitcher **Claude Jonnard** (brother of Bubber Jonnard) would also go the Giants. The New York Giants let him pitch four innings at the end of this season. He would go for additional short stays in 1922, 1923 and 1924. The St. Louis Browns would look him in 1926 and the Chicago Cubs would give him a look in 1929. His major league record ended at 13-12 but he pitched 350 games in six seasons, including facing nine batters in two World Series. On the negative side in threw 1,923 wild pitches. He led the National League in saves in 1922 and 1923. He was second in 1924. (going)[105]; **Hank Robinson,** another native Arkansan pitcher, also did well in the majors. He played for the Pittsburgh Pirates in 1911-1913. In 1914 and 1915 he hurled for the St. Louis Cardinals, and in 1918 played for the New York Yankees. His record was 42-37 in the majors. He maintained a 2.53 ERA (coming); Leo **Dickerman** also was destined to appear in the major leagues. In 1923 he would get the call from the Brooklyn Robins and pitch 159 games. He would split 1924 between the Robins and the St. Louis Cardinals. In 1925 he pitched 15 games for the Cards winning only four of them. His major league file would close with a 19-37 record. His crowning achievement was pitching two shutouts in the 1924 season. He returned to the minors and pitched until 1927. (going)[106]

5. **Memphis Chicasaws:** The Memphis Chicasaws (also known as "The Chicks") is a team that would play a pivotal role in **Cy Warmoth's** future. It too hosted a lot of talent in fielding, batting and pitching and major league scouts were watching them frequently. On this team were several past and future major leaguers. They included the old veteran **Tommy McMillan.** He played shortstop

---

[104] http://www.baseball-reference.com/players/j/jackstr01.shtml
[105] http://www.baseball-reference.com/players/j/jonnacl01.shtml
[106] http://www.baseball-reference.com/players/d/dickele01.shtml

and center field. He started his career with The Brooklyn Superbas in 1908 and played there in 1909 and part of 1910. He played 82 games for the Cincinnati Reds. In 1912 he played for the New York Highlanders. In those four seasons he appeared at the plate 1,114 times in 297 games.(coming)[107]; Third baseman **Rinaldo Williams** played in four games for the Brooklyn Tiptops of the Federal League in 1914. (coming); **Howie Camp** had the privilege of playing five games with the 1917 New York Yankees. There were several notables on that Yankee team including the legends Urban Shocker, Home Run Baker, and Muddy Ruel.(coming).[108]; **Oscar Tuero** pitched three seasons for the St. Louis Cardinals. He must have pitched mostly relief. His record was 5-8 but he worked 199 innings in those two years. Tuero was born in Havana Cuba (coming). [109] **Paul Zahniser** would join **Cy Warmoth** on the pitching staff of the Washington Nationals in 1923. He would stay again in 1924, the year of the great Nationals World Series victory but he would not play. He spent 1925 and 1926 with the Boston Red Sox. In 1929 he played one game and pitched one inning for the Cincinnati Red Legs.(going)[110]. He returned to the minors and pitched until 1937.(going). **Handy Andy High** played second and third base and shortstop. The majors called him in 1922. He played with the Brooklyn Robins 1922-1924, He split 1925 between the Robins and the Boston Braves. He stayed with the Robins in 1926 and 1927. In 1928 his services went to the St. Louis Cardinals, where he stayed thru 1931; 1932 and 1933 were spent with the Cincinnati Red Legs. He ended his major league career with the Philadelphia Phillies in 1934. He played in 1,166 games. He had 42 home runs, 482 RBIs and turned in a respectable .284 batting average. He also played in three World Series while at St. Louis. (going)[111]; **Bernie "Bud" Hungllng** had a three year stay in the majors. He spent 1922 and 1923 with the Brooklyn Robins. He would then retire to the minors until 1930 when he would get a call up from the St. Louis Browns at age 34. He was a catcher and

---

[107] http://www.baseball-reference.com/players/m/mcmilto01.shtml
[108] http://www.baseball-reference.com/players/c/campho01.shtml
[109] http://www.baseball-reference.com/players/t/tueroos01.shtml
[110] http://www.baseball-reference.com/players/z/zahnipa01.shtml
[111] http://www.baseball-reference.com/players/h/highan01.shtml

played in 51 games. He hit one major league home run in 1922. His batting average was .231 (going)[112] **Howard "Polly" McLarry**, first and second baseman, got the nod from the Chicago White Sox in 1912. He played in two games and batted twice and did not hit. In 1915 the Chicago Cubs called him back and he played in 68 games. He hit 25 times and stole two bases. He returned to the minors and played until 1928 (coming).[113]

6. **Mobile Bears:** The 1921 Mobile Bears team was not exactly talent laden for the majors. The big star of this class would be catcher **Johnny Schulte**, a native of Fredericktown Maryland. He would get a brief stay from the St. Louis Browns in 1923, catching in seven games. In 1927 at the age of 30, the St. Louis Cardinals would call him back. He did much better this round. He played in 64 games and slugged nine home runs and knocked in 32 runners. His average was a strong .288. He probably caught several games for the legendary Pete Alexander who was ending his career and not far from death's door (going)[114] **Walt Golvin,** first baseman, played two games for the Cubs in 1922 with no invitation to stay (going); Third Baseman **Billy Mullen** played a total of 36 major league games for three teams between 1920 and 1928 but did not get an invitation to hang around. Right handed pitcher **Ray Roberts** pitched in two games for the Philadelphia Athletics in 1919 without good result. **Red Torkelson,** another right hander, hurled three games for Cleveland in 1917. Ironically he won two of them but was not offered a job.(coming)[115];

7. **Nashville Volunteers:** (Cy Warmoth's New Teammates) Nashville had a pair of old timers for guidance. **Tony Tonneman,** 39, and **Hugh "Corns" Bradley**.36. Tonneman had a partial season with Boston in 1911. He caught two games (coming) Bradley played a total of 225 games in the majors. He got his first chance with Boston in 1910-1912. He played catcher, first base and outfield. He then jumped to the Federal League and played for the Pittsburgh Rebels in 1914. He split 1915 between the Rebels, the Brooklyn Tiptops and the Newark Peppers. All but 27 of his appearances he

---

[112] http://www.baseball-reference.com/players/h/hunglbe01.shtml
[113] http://www.baseball-reference.com/players/m/mclarpo01.shtml
[114] http://www.baseball-reference.com/minors/player.cgi?id=schult002joh
[115] http://www.baseball-reference.com/players/t/torkere01.shtml

played first base. His batting average in the American League was only .203 but was a respectable .314 for his lifetime. (coming);[116] **Bubber Jonnard** caught one game for the Chicago White Sox in 1920. In 1922 he caught 10 games for the Pirates. He played 56 games for the Phillies in 1926-27. In 1929 he caught 18 games for the St. Louis Cardinals. Strangely in 1935 at age 37 he caught one more game for the Phillies.(going)[117]; Right hander **George Payne** was given a chance to pitch by the Chicago White Sox. In 12 outings he won half his games but was never called back by the White Sox or any other team.(coming)[118] **Red Lucas** was only 19 years old in 1921 but he had a bright future as a pitcher. He would get brief looks from the Giants and Red Sox in 1923 and 1924. He would become a starter for the Cincinnati Red Legs in 1926 and stay with them for seven more seasons. In 1934 he would pass to the Pirates and complete five seasons for them. In his lifetime he would play in 396 games and win 157 of them. He started 302 games. He would have a lifetime ERA of 3.72. He was nominated to the Hall of Fame but never selected.(going)[119]; Also on that team was another pitcher who had been to the big show. **Hub Perdue** pitched five seasons in the majors. From 1912 to part of 1914 he pitched for the Boston Red Sox. The rest of 1914 and part of 1915 he pitched for the St. Louis Cardinals. While his career was not a long one, he won 51 games while losing 64. He had a few Hall of Fame votes. In 1938 and 1939 but, of course, was not selected. He had several appearances on the National League Leader Boards during his playing days.

8. **The New Orleans Pelicans** team of 1921 could have been mistaken for Major League Baseball's hatchery. Seven of nine New Orleans pitchers would make it to the majors. **Eddie Matteson,** at age 36, had the briefest of appearances. He was 3-2 at Philadelphia in 1914. In 1918 he had a 5-3 record for the Nationals. He pitched 125 games.(coming); **Abraham Lincoln "Sweetbread" Bailey** had a 4-7 record in the majors. He pitched 137 innings of baseball, mostly for the Chicago Cubs. The Brooklyn Robins used him 24

---

[116] http://www.baseball-reference.com/players/b/bradlhu01.shtml
[117] http://www.baseball-reference.com/players/j/jonnabu01.shtml
[118] http://www.baseball-reference.com/players/p/paynege01.shtml
[119] http://www.baseball-reference.com/players/l/lucasre01.shtml

innings in 1924 (going). **Hal Goldsmith** would tryout for Boston and St. Louis (1926-29) but not shine enough to stay. His record 6-10 (going)[120]; **Lefty James** tried out for Cleveland in 1912, 1913 and 1914 and had a 2-7 record; **John Martina** is a strange case in major league baseball. He would start 14 games in his Major League Career His record was 6-8 for the Washington Nationals. He would, however, play one inning in the 1924 World Series facing three batters. He appeared in Game Three of the Series. Washington would use four pitchers in this game but lose to the New York Giants 6-4. (going)[121]; **Tom Phillips** was another Pelican with brief shots at making the big time. He had a 1-3 record for the St. Louis Browns in 1915. In 1919 he would earn a 3-2 record for the Cleveland Indians. The Washington Nationals would look at him for a single game in 1921. He would pitch another game for them in 1922. His major league record was 8-12 (going)[122]; The surprise pitcher on the Pelican team would be a power pitcher named **Dazzy Vance**. He was big for the era, measuring 6-2 in height and weighing in at 200 pounds. The Yankees and Pirates first looked at him in 1915 but offered no contracts. The New York Yankees called him back in 1918 and let him pitch two innings. Still they offered him no contract. But the worm turned in 1922 when the Brooklyn Robins gave him a job. He stayed with them for 11 more seasons, amassing a 190-131 record. He then went to the St. Louis Cardinals in 1933 and pitched eight games and establishing a 6-2 record. He split 1934 between the Cincinnati Red Legs and the Cardinals. He finished in 1935 pitching five more games for Brooklyn. For 16 seasons in the majors he established a record of 197 wins and 140 losses. His lifetime ERA was 3.24. He pitched in the 1934 World Series when the Cardinals beat Detroit. He was elected to the **Baseball Hall of Fame** in 1955. Not only Pelican pitchers went to the majors. There were others of talent on the 1921 team as well. **Red Sheridan** played five games for Brooklyn in 1918 and 1920. He hit once in seven trips to the plate.(coming); **Don Rader,** shortstop, leftfielder and third baseman appeared in four games for the Chicago White Sox in 1913. Before this season

---

[120] http://www.baseball-reference.com/players/g/goldsha01.shtml
[121] http://www.baseball-reference.com/players/m/martijo02.shtml
[122] http://www.baseball-reference.com/players/p/phillto01.shtml

ended he would get called up again by the Philadelphia Phillies. He would play in nine games and hit nine times in 36 appearances for a respectable .281 batting average. Unfortunately he would not be invited to stay (going)[123]. **Bert Griffith**, outfielder, would get a more extended stay. The Brooklyn Robins would use him in 106 games in the 1922 season. He belted an impressive 100 hits in 344 trips to the plate. Among those hits were two homers, eight triples and 22 doubles. The Robins would hold him over another year and he would appear only 79 times at the plate but his batting average would only drop to .294 (compared to .308 the previous season). We don't know why, but he was traded to The Washington Nationals in 1924 but he only played in two games. He never went back to the majors.[124] (going); **Hank Deberry**, catcher, would have a longer life in the majors. He was first called up at the ripe old age of 21 by the Cleveland Indians. He spent two seasons there playing 40 games and managing a decent .273 batting average both seasons. He was released and returned to the minors. He would get a final call up in 1922 by the Brooklyn Robins. He would stay there until 1930 when he would leave with a batting average of .267. He consistently appeared on the National League leader boards[125]. (going); **Roy Leslie** played seven games for the Chicago Cubs in 1917 and 12 games for the St. Louis Cardinals in 1919. Neither tryout was impressive. However in 1922 at age 27 he would don his catching equipment for the Philadelphia Phillies in 141 games. His batting average would blossom to .271 and he would hit six home runs. Unfortunately it would be his last year in the majors (going)[126]. **Ike Boone** was another minor leaguer who would find his way in the majors. His start would be a meager two games for the Giants in 1922 and another five for Boston in 1922. But in 1924 the Red Sox would invite him back and give him starting status. He would stay with them until traded to the Chicago White Sox in 1927 where he only played in 11 games. Brooklyn would use him in 27 games in 1930 and eight games in 1932. In 1924 he was rated as one of the top ten sluggers in the

---

[123] http://www.baseball-reference.com/players/r/raderdo01.shtml
[124] http://www.baseball-reference.com/players/g/griffbe01.shtml
[125] http://www.baseball-reference.com/players/d/deberha01.shtml
[126] http://www.baseball-reference.com/players/l/lesliro01.shtml

American League[127] (going). **Larry Gilbert** played two seasons for the Boston Braves in 1914 and 1915. A right-fielder, he sported a .230 batting average.[128] (coming).[129].

It appears **Cy Warmoth** was a primary hurler for the Nashville Volunteers. His player-coach Bubba Jonnard appears to have caught 127 games for the Volunteers and Cy is listed as have pitched 38 games. He is listed as having a record of 18 wins and 20 losses (38 games). Right-handed pitcher George Payne had a 10-19 record. Frank Lankanau had a 10-5 record for the third most games played. Apparently Cy, even though a lefthander, was the workhorse for the Volunteers. His ERA was 3.76. Cy's hitting was a weak .183.

It should be noted that in a league of six teams, opposing batters get to know a pitcher pretty well by the end of the season. His earned run average (ERA) was 3.76. While some might think that a little bit high, it was well lower than other Travelers pitchers. Frank Lankenau, who only pitched 15 games, was closest at 3.94. The other pitchers exceeded 5 runs per game.

Apparently the Volunteers' home field contributed to the high number of runs scored. The most peculiar features of the field was that uphill outfield slope. The fences were short and right field was also an overflow place for large crowds. The story of Sulphur Dell is told in many places on The Internet but one of the best I have found is the story told by Warren Corbett at the website: http://bioproj.sabr.org/bioproj.cfm?a=v&v=l&bid=2044&pid=19558. Here is an excerpt from the story:

> "Right field resembled a ridiculously short par-three hole on a golf course, with the tee at home plate, shooting at a tiny elevated green just a 79-yard chip shot away. The base of the fence—262 feet down the foul line—stood 25 feet above the infield. The slope began gradually a few steps behind the first baseman, and then shot up at a 45-degree angle. It leveled off 235 feet out, forming a ten-foot-wide shelf. Then the 45-degree climb resumed to the fence.
>
> Nashville right fielders were called "mountain goats." They usually grazed on the terrace so they could run downhill for short pop-ups

---

[127] http://www.baseball-reference.com/players/b/booneik01.shtml
[128] http://www.baseball-reference.com/players/g/gilbela01.shtml
[129] http://www.baseball-reference.com/players/b/booneik01.shtml

and ground balls. To negotiate the hillside, former goat Bob Lennon said, "You got to know how to run with the short leg and the long leg."

This topography produced more low comedy than high drama. According an often-repeated tale, Smead Jolley (a professional minor leaguer 1922-1941), always an accident waiting to happen in the outfield, fought the Dump and lost in his first game there in 1937. Jolley chugged down the embankment to pick up a ground-ball single, but it skipped between his legs and rolled up to the fence. He whirled to handle the carom as the ball gathered speed on its return trip downhill. That, too, eluded him. By the time he subdued the ball the batter was rounding third. Jolley uncorked a strong throw—so strong it overshot the catcher. The hitter scored and Jolley was charged with three errors on the play."[130]

The Dell was also known for its fragrances. The ball field was built on the site of a natural sulfur water spring. A city dump was nearby and the park was sometimes flooded by big rains which caused the Cumberland River to overflow. Throw in the smell of cigarettes, cigars and popcorn and you have potpourri only a true baseball fan would enjoy,

Pitchers are usually not relied on for their hitting ability. Cy hit 20 singles and three doubles in 48 trips to the plate, yet his batting average was a weak .183.

We don't know how many batters Cy faced in the 285 innings he pitched for the Volunteers but the records indicate he issued 151 walks and allowed 306 hits. He was 28 years old this season, still a young age for a professional baseball player in 1921.[131]

---

[130] http://bioproj.sabr.org/bioproj.cfm?a=v&v=l&bid=2044&pid=19558
[131] http://www.baseball-reference.com/minors/team.cgi?id=26074

# CHAPTER 9

# Now a Traveler

## 1922—Part 1

SUDDENLY IT WAS another season and Cy Warmoth found himself with orders to report to another team in the Southern Association League. His new team was the Little Rock, Arkansas Travelers.

Prospects, he surely knew, were not pleasant. The Southern League had again been shook up by the annual player trades. Claude Jonnard went to Indianapolis to play AA ball. Leo Dickerman shifted over to the Memphis Chickasaws. Conrad Fields went over to Nashville where Cy had been. A couple of fill-in pitchers were also out of the lineup. Between the trades in the minors and the comings and going from the majors, the Southern Association League rivaled a Methodist Minister's Reassignment Conference in actvity.

Cy and a fellow Illinoisan pitcher, Mike Svengros from Pana, Illinois would be shouldering much of the southpaw duties. Mutt Williams, a right-handed 20-19 pitcher had also been brought in from the Texas Leagues.

Little did Cy know that before this year ended, he would get another call from the Major Leagues but before that there would be a major accident marring his professional baseball life.

Gilbert "Gil" Meyers was having his best year yet in the minors. He had just arrived to wear the Nashville colors. It was his fourth season catching in the Southern Association. The 33$^{rd}$ game would be his last in baseball. While we do not know the details of the play, Meyers was spiked above the ankle, severing a tendon, in a play at first base. It happened in June. Cy Warmoth was the person who spiked him. The incident is recorded on the history of The Sulphur Dell Ball Park previously referenced.[132]

Spikes on baseball shoes, thank goodness, have left the ball fields to be replaced by hard rubber cleats which are not so dangerous. In early

---

[132] http://www.sulphurdell.com/Timeline_.htm

American baseball, where base stealing was a really important part of the game, speed was essential. The use of spikes began in the 1800's when, to improve speed, baseball players had blacksmiths attach sharp spikes to the toes and heels of their shoes. The purpose was speed but in reality they became offensive weapons. The official rules of baseball "Section 21 drawn up in 1860 clearly stated:

> "If the player is prevented from making a base, by the intentional obstruction of an adversary, he shall be entitled to that base, and not put out."
>
> This, combined with Section 19 ("Players running the bases must, so far as possible, keep upon a direct line between the bases; and, should any player run three feet out of this line, for the purpose of avoiding the ball in the hands of an adversary, he shall be declared out.")

These rules set the stage for open warfare by base runners. Baseball runners have been fiercely protecting that right ever since. Thus began the time honored adage: "The base line belongs to the runner."

Spiking incidents in early baseball were commonplace. Base runners were extremely aggressive in base stealing. Ty Cobb stole more than 800 bases in his career. He also gained a reputation as someone who would hurt an opposing player if he could. He vigorously denied the allegations in his book *My Life in Baseball-The True Record*. He was nearly kicked out of baseball concerning an alleged spiking incident with Frank "Home Run" Baker. It was only publication of a photograph of the slide that cleared him from the charges. Fans had threatened to kill him over the incident before the photo was published.

Baseball teams in even earlier years faced another danger from spiking. In those days many teams were known by the color of their stockings rather than the emblems on their uniforms. Stockings were thought to have protected the legs of base runners and added a great deal of color to their appearance. Thus there were many teams named for their stocking colors, including the Cincinnati Red Legs and the Boston Red Stockings. It was learned through misfortune that the dyes used to color those stockings could be lethal in an open wound such as a 5/8-1" spike puncture might cause. The National League banished the colored stockings in 1907 after a rash of infections attributed to the dyes in the stockings. (Another discussion could be had about the cleanliness of the spikes themselves.)[133] Many teams, according to The Society for American Baseball Research, Inc. in their publication, *The National PasTime No. 10*, had begun replace the stockings with more white sanitary stockings in 1910.

Cy Warmoth's spiking of Gil Meyers was probably unintentional, as were many of the incidents which plagued ball players in the early years. It is almost certain the thought of ending the career of a fellow ball player, accidental or not, would carry some emotional weight. It was also a reminder of the mortal danger all players faced. Cy had been a Nashville Volunteer and both were members of the same League—although they were never teammates—and likely encountered each other many times. A ligament in Meyer's lower leg was severed. The description of the wound location makes it sound like a "stepping" accident such as would occur when an infielder and a base runner arrived at a base at the same time.

Cy determinedly continued on the first leg of his 1922 journey. This year the home park would be Kavanaugh Field. It was originally constructed at what was called West End Park. Judge William Kavanaugh, owner of the Traveler team, and also president of the Southern Association League, died suddenly in 1915. The field was renamed in his honor. In many ways it was a typical stadium of the minor leagues. It was a wooden grandstand that seated 3,500 fans. It was later revamped to seat 4,500 spectators. Several northern teams, including the Boston Red Sox, considered making it a Spring Training facility. Meager though it was by today's standards, the field was home to two Hall of Famers, one of them Cy's new Teammate Travis "Stonewall" Jackson. The other was Bill Dickey.[134]

**Travis Jackson,** short stop and third baseman, would play for the Travs for almost the entire season of 1922 but would get a 3-game tryout for the New York Giants. He must have done well for they invited him back in 1923 and he stayed with them for 14 full seasons. He had a lifetime BA of .291 and appeared in the 1934 All Star Game. He was elected to the Baseball Hall of Fame in 1982.[135]

**Bill Dickey** would start his professional career in Little Rock in 1926, playing only 61 games. He spent the other half of the season in Muskogee,

---

[133] http://research.sabr.org/journals/files/SABR-National_Pastime-10.pdf
[134] http://ballparks.baseballyakker.com/?page_id=120
[135] http://encyclopediaofarkansas.net/encyclopedia/entry-detail.aspx?entryID=673

Oklahoma playing with the Western Association. He played 61 games there. The boy was a slugger and the New York Yankees soon heard about him. His first year in the Southern Association he batted .302. In his stay at Little Rock he batted .391, including 18 hits, a double and five triples in 60 games. He came back to play another 60 games in 1928 and again in 1948 for eight games. A catcher, he would spend 17 seasons with the New York Yankees, teaming up with the legends Lou Gehrig and Babe Ruth. He was elected to the Hall of Fame in 1954. *To the best our knowledge he never crossed paths with Cy Warmoth.*[136]

Baseball history, meager though it is, indicates that Cy's experience in the Southern Association was not golden, nor was it disastrous. The veteran Hank Robinson, the "old man" of the team at age 34, won 26 games while losing only 11 for an impressive .703 average. The young Mike Svengros was 17-14 for .548. A couple of other pitchers had .500 or better but they didn't pitch many games. Cy, now 29 years old, won 17 and lost 22. Of the three workhorses on the pitching staff, he also had the worst ERA. His average was 3.77, (not to insinuate that keeping the opponents to an average of less than four runs per game in several short field ballparks was terrible). He was also last of the three for hitting, but most clubs would be happy to have a pitcher hitting .257. All three of the pitchers were going most of the way in their games and a lot of relief pitching was not being used. Based on the records posted by Baseballreference.com, Cy would have been averaging 8.025 innings per game

Out of the blue, whatever the reason, Cy got called to the front office of the Travs. Would he be interested in going back to the Washington Nationals for another major league tryout? Indeed he would. He "hobo-ed" his personal baseball bats and trusty glove, grabbed his civvies and headed for the nation's capitol. He was ready for another glimpse of glory and probably thought just watching the seemingly immortal Walter Johnson pitch would make the trip worthwhile.

---

[136] http://encyclopediaofarkansas.net/encyclopedia/entry-detail.aspx?entryID=645

# CHAPTER 10

# A Second Chance At The Majors

## Fall 1922

MAYBE IT WAS true what the old vaudeville comedians said about the Nationals: "First in war, first in peace, and last in the American League." Even if the Nationals were not in the league basement, they were usually close enough to feel the draft. This puzzled many fans because the Nats had some great players. The Nationals just could not put together a great season. They were perceived as a sorry franchise. Oddly, it was because they lost so many baseball games they found a home in the American League.

The American League came into being because the old National League of which they were a member decided to reduce its roster to eight teams from the original 12. Four teams that were winning less than half their games (Washington, Baltimore, Cleveland and Louisville) were arbitrarily cut from the schedule. The league ostensibly made this cutback to help get better control over the league processes and to improve profitability. The truth was the NL had little (almost lost) control over its member teams on such fundamental issues as scheduling and team stability. So they thought they could manage and control eight teams better than a dozen.[137]

The new American league came about primarily through the efforts of a young man named Ban Johnson, an Ohio native, who became friendly with Charles Comiskey who was at that time the manager of the Cincinnati Reds and through "Commy" and a few other owners had gotten himself appointed Commissioner of the Western League.

Johnson, a former sports reporter, had long been critical of the rowdy atmosphere which had invaded and then pervaded organized baseball at the start of the 20th century. Johnson argued that fighting, abusive language, and abuse of umpires were hurting attendance because women and children were being kept at home. Johnson contended baseball had always been, and

---

[137] http://en.wikipedia.org/wiki/American_League

should always be, a family spectator sport. When made commissioner of the Western League he introduced, among other innovations, player fines for fighting, foul language and abuse of umpires. His "clean up" measures and empowerment of umpires to eject players and coaches, worked immediate wonders and the Western League was soon recognized as the best managed league in the country.[138]

When the National League reduced its membership Ban Johnson, Comiskey and others moved with dispatch to create a brand new American League in 1900. Technically it was still a minor league franchise of the National League. The following year it withdrew from what was called The National Agreement and declared itself a second major league. The NL owners then compounded their stupid mistake with another and announced a salary cap of $2,400 on all players. It was an obvious attempt to thwart player salary growth.

Johnson and the new AL managers went to work. Soon they had signed many of the National Leagues best players.

Most responsible for signing 39 NL players was Clark "The Old Fox" Griffith. Griffith, who would be elected to the Hall of Fame in 1955, had started in professional baseball in 1891 as a pitcher for the St. Louis Browns. He came up through the "dead ball" era in Chicago teams (Colts, Orphans, White Sox) before graduating to player manager positions for the New York Highlanders (Yankees) before coming to Washington in the same role in 1912. (Note: Griffith had a ten percent ownership with The Nationals when he arrived in 1912. He had officially ended his playing role by the time he became partners with William Richardson in 1919. Richardson, a Philadelphia grain broker, mortgaged a Montana ranch to buy another 40 percent of the franchise. The deal allowed Griffith the right to act as manager of the club.)[139]

Griffith was trying hard to turn the fortunes of the Nationals around and had no luck as of the approaching end of the 1922 season. Thus, the club, which was operating on the proverbial shoestring, needed to find and recruit cheap new talent. *Cy Warmoth was a possibility.*

## Saturday: September 16, 1922:

In mid September when the Washington Senators rolled into Michigan Central Station in Detroit, Wallace Walter Warmoth walked into a new

---

[138] http://en.wikipedia.org/wiki/Ban_Johnson
[139] http://en.wikipedia.org/wiki/Clark_Griffith

world. Detroit was bustling and commerce investments loomed throughout the city. Michigan Central (also called Michigan Central Depot and MCS) was not yet ten years old. Navin Field, later to be called Tiger Stadium, was older than the elegant train station. Navin was the second stadium to be built at the corner of Trumbull and Michigan. The original, Bennett Stadium, a wooden grandstand built and expanded to accommodate 18,000 fans, was torn down after the 1911 season and replaced with a concrete-steel structure. The Tigers played their first game at Navin Field April 20, 1912 when it could seat 23,000 fans. There were already plans to renovate it and the following season it would be enlarged to accommodate 30,000. The field was accentuated with a 54-foot backstop and a 125-foot flag pole. If the ball hit the pole, the ball was still in play. It was 440-feet to deep center, 340 feet to the left field bleachers and 325-feet to right.[140]

The Senators were returning from winning two of three games off the Cleveland Indians and now they had arrived at the House of Cobb for a three-day trial. Manager Jesse Clyde "Deerfoot" Milan got Cy into the first game of the series. Milan was culminating 16 seasons of playing for Washington. He never played for another major league team and this would also be his only year as a manager. As a player he showed steadfastness and tremendous footwork. When his career ended he would have stolen 495 bases, batted 7,359 times and retire with a batting average of .285. He followed George McBride as player manager. McBride was fired after an 80-73 season. They both followed Clark Griffith, the current club president. Milan had left Cleveland (the last opponent of the waning season) with a 61-74 record, so he knew his future as manager was in doubt.

The Saturday game featured the Nats' Ray Francis pitching against the Tigers' Red Oldham. Neither pitcher had a winning record. Francis held his own until the fifth inning when the Tigers' bats found pay dirt. He gave up 9 hits and seven runs before Milan jerked him out. He opted for a left-hander and sent Cy to the mound. Cy faced three batters, walking one, before Milan replaced him with Erick Erickson who was 4-12 on the season. Erickson finished the inning and then turned the ball over to Jim Brillheart, a Radford, Virginia boy the front office had great hopes for. Brillheart held the line but the lead could not be overcome. The final score was Detroit 9 Washington 5.[141]

---

[140] http://www.ballparksofbaseball.com/past/TigerStadium.htm
[141] http://www.baseball-reference.com/boxes/DET/DET192209160.shtml

The next day George Mogridge pitched all nine innings and won the game 6-2 and improved his record to 16-12.

## Monday, September 18, 1922:

Cy's second relief opportunity in the majors finally came on Monday September 18, 1922. The Tigers won the final game of the series, annihilating three Washington pitchers, including Cy. Brillheart pitched four innings and gave up as many runs. Tom Zachary relieved for one inning and gave up another four runs. Cy stayed in for three innings and gave up six hits, walked one batter while committing three errors. He struck no one out. Three runs scored during his tour of duty. On the brighter offensive side of the game he batted once, scored a hit and then got knocked in and scored a run. His major league BA was now 1.000. The final score was 11-5. He probably left Detroit feeling like Babe Ruth.

The records don't show exactly whom he faced, but because he faced 15 batters, it's probably a good bet he met the entire starting lineup except for the starting pitcher Syl Johnson. He probably faced Red Oldham. It was an interesting twist of irony, for fate had plans for Cy and Red. Here are the other players on that strong Detroit team

1. (1B): **Fred "Pudge" Haney** was in his Rookie year. He was averaging one hit per game and batting above .300. [142]
2. (3B): **Bob "Ducky" Jones** wasn't the Tigers' primary power hitter per se, but he was fast and sneaky and on the top ten leader board for sacrifices. He had plenty of doubles and triples to his credit this season.[143]
3. (CF): **Ty Cobb**, always dangerous[144]
4. (LF): **Bobby Veach**, also batting over .300 and in the top five of the league for runs batted in.[145]
5. (RF): **Bob Fothergill** was next. This was his first year but he too had joined the .300 club.[146]
6. (2B): **George "Cutty" Cutshaw** was another wily old veteran. He had been hammering pitchers in the majors since 1912. He had

---

[142] http://www.baseball-reference.com/managers/haneyfr01.shtml
[143] http://www.baseball-reference.com/players/j/jonesbo01.shtml
[144] http://www.baseball-reference.com/players/c/cobbty01.shtml
[145] http://www.baseball-reference.com/players/v/veachbo01.shtml
[146] http://www.baseball-reference.com/players/f/fothebo01.shtml

been in only one World Series. He was a base stealer, having a career total in excess of 250. His batting average was in the .250 neighborhood.[147]
7. (SS): **Topper Rigney** was a Texas rookie who seemed to be a hitting phenomenon. He was averaging at least one single per game. Often he followed his singles up with an extra-base.[148]
8. (CAT): **Johnny Bassler**: Hit .298 the previous year and was well ahead of his pace the year before.[149]
9. (P) **Slyester "Syl" Johnson** showed no Babe Ruth-like propensities. His current pitching record was 10-6 but his BA a meager .181[150]
10. (RP) **Red Oldham**, born in Zion, Maryland in 1893, played in 29 games for Detroit in 1914 and 1915. He then spent some developmental time in the Pacific and International leagues before returning to Detroit in 1920. After the 1922 season he would make brief appearances for the Pittsburgh Pirates in 1925-1926 before going back to the minors.

When the game was over, the team hustled to the train headed on a long trip south. They were headed for St. Louis. On September 19, 1922 Cy got a treat as he watched 34-year old Walter Johnson win a game. He probably watched closely as "The Big Train" threw hard and fast. Johnson threw so fast that many who faced him swore they never saw the ball. It would have been a fascinating game to see. St Louis' Elam Vangilder was closing in on 20 wins.

Johnson was almost as important to the City of Washington as the White House. He was one of the baseball team's few claims to fame. Even fans in other cities loved Johnson. Born in Kansas in November 1887, he moved with his family to California at age 14. He had come to the Nationals via a scout who saw him pitching in the Idaho State League. At age 19 he established a 5-9 record but Washington recognized his potential and kept the ruddy faced boy. By age 22 the investment began to pay off. He went 25-17 in 1910. From that point he just kept re-writing pitching history.

Johnson had unusually long arms and a hybrid submariner style of delivery. It was apparently easy on his arm, because he lasted long enough

---

[147] http://www.baseball-reference.com/players/c/cutshge01.shtml
[148] http://www.baseball-reference.com/players/r/rigneto01.shtml
[149] http://www.baseball-reference.com/players/b/bassljo01.shtml
[150] http://www.baseball-reference.com/players/j/johnssy01.shtml

to face 23,405 batters, pitch 113 shutouts and win 20 or more games in 12 seasons. His best record was in 1913 when he went 36-7. By 1922 he was reaching the end of his career. It was obvious to those who followed him that he was slipping. Now he was 34-years old, only five years older than Cy.[151]

Cy should have felt better when he saw both Walter Johnson and Vangilder were human. Johnson's game, although he pitched all nine innings, was anything but perfect. He gave up eight hits, committed three errors and allowed two home runs. Johnson didn't walk anyone. Vangilder lasted eight innings. He allowed 10 hits, committed four errors and struck out two hitters. He put Johnson on base when he hit him with a pitch. Ray Kolp came in to try and save him in the ninth. It was futile. When the smoke cleared, Washington won the first game of this series 4-3. It was Johnson's 15th win against 15 losses for the year.[152]

The next day, Wednesday, September 20, Ray Francis came in and pitched a 4-hitter and the Nationals blanked the second place Browns 5-0. If nothing else, Cy should have learned that he had a heck of a team to help him.[153] The losing pitcher was another legend in the making. Urban Shocker is one of the most talked and written about players of the era. It is surprising his numbers never got him into the Hall of Fame. He was nominated five times.[154]

## **Thursday September 21, 1922:**

On paper it would seem the Senator's had a darned good chance to win this one. Cy wouldn't have known it then but this maligned and losing team he was playing for was loaded with stars. Many of the players who warmed up on the field with him would be baseball legends. The Washington starting lineup:

1. (1B), **Joe Judge:** Completed 20 seasons in the Major Leagues, all but three with the Washington Nationals. Nominated seven times for Hall of Fame but not selected. Appeared at the plate over 9,100 times, lifetime BA .298; played in 14 World Series games.[155]

---

[151] Lawrence Ritter & Donald Honig, *The 100 Greatest Baseball Players of All Time,* Crown Publishers, Inc., New York. pp. 241
[152] http://www.baseball-reference.com/boxes/SLA/SLA192209190.shtml
[153] http://www.baseball-reference.com/boxes/SLA/SLA192209200.shtml
[154] http://www.baseball-reference.com/players/s/shockur01.shtml
[155] http://www.baseball-reference.com/players/j/judgejo01.shtml

2. **(2B) Bucky Harris** Hall of Fame (1975). 12 seasons in majors, last 2 with the Detroit Tigers, the rest with the Nationals. Involved in 3,412 putouts. Paid $7,000 in 1924, the year the Nationals won the World Series. Went up to $30,000 in 25-26-27 under player-manager contract.[156]
3. (RF) **Sam Rice**: Elected to Hall of Fame in 1963. He spent 20 seasons in the majors, all but one with the Nationals. He went to Cleveland his last year. He appeared at the plate 10,246 times and a lifetime batting average of .322.[157]
4. (LF) **Goose Goslin**: Played 18 seasons in MLB with 9,822 Plate Appearances, BA .316. 12 years with Nationals, also played for Detroit and the St. Louis Browns. Went to the All Star Game in 1936. Elected to Hall of Fame in 1968.Career BA .316. Putouts 4,792. (Washington paid him $16,000 in 1929).[158]
5. (RF) **Howie Shanks**: Came to the majors in 1912 and played in 1,665 games before leaving in 1925. He spent most of his days with Washington but finished with Boston and New York. He was a solid player hitting .251 as a lifetime BA.[159]
6. **Pete Lapan** (CAT): Pete had also come up from Little Rock and this was his tryout. The Nationals had worked him steady this year and he was batting above .300[160]
7. (SS) **Roger Peckinbaugh**: Signed by the Cleveland Naps in 1910. Played for Yankees 1913-1921. Came to work for Nationals in 1922 (same as Cy). He signed for $2,400 in 1914. By 1918 the Yankees were paying him $5,500 The Nationals paid him $12,500 in 1926. Won AL MVP in 1925.
8. (3B) **Bobby LaMotte**: LaMotte played 5 seasons in the majors. He and Cy would team up again in 1924 in the minors.[161]
9. (P) **George Mogridge**: Mogridge pitched 265 ML games in 15 seasons and won nearly half of them. He had 678 strikeouts to his career. He won one game in the 1924 season.

---

[156] http://www.baseball-reference.com/managers/harribu01.shtml
[157] http://www.baseball-reference.com/players/r/ricesa01.shtml
[158] http://www.baseball-reference.com/players/g/gosligo01.shtml
[159] http://www.baseball-reference.com/players/s/shankho01.shtml
[160] http://www.baseball-reference.com/players/l/lapanpe01.shtml
[161] http://www.baseball-reference.com/players/l/lamotbo01.shtml

There was another hornet nest waiting for Cy on this afternoon. By the end of the second inning it was evident, George Mogridge, a 34-year-old lefty, wasn't going to get his 17th win today. The Browns came out with bats blazing and Manager Milan jerked Mogridge and replaced him with Jim Brillheart after the first out in the third inning. Brillheart gave up seven hits, three runs and added two errors to the four made by Mogridge. He faced 17 batters in a little more than three innings.

From the bullpen in Sportsman's Park III where he waited, Cy could still admire and evaluate the Browns lineup. It looked like this:

(RF) **Jack Tobin** got his start in the Federal League with the St. Louis Terriers. He could be counted on as a .300 plus hitter since settling in with the Browns. (Tobin retired with a .302 BA in 1927. He played thirteen major league seasons.)[162]

(3B) **Eddie Foster**: "The Kid" (his nickname) usually had his name on the top ten boards for good reasons. He led the "at bats" category in the American League in 1912, 1914, 1915 and 1918. He finished second in 1916. Foster came into the big show in 1910, playing 22 games for the New York Highlanders (Yankees). In 1912 the Nationals picked him up and played him in 154 games. He stayed with the Nationals until they traded him to the Red Sox along with Harry Harper and Mike Menosky in January 1920 for Braggo Roth and Red Shannon. Neither of those players were still with Washington. St. Louis had picked Foster up on waivers just a few days before (August 15). He was now 35 years old and probably near to the end of his career. (Foster was nominated to the Baseball Hall of Fame in 1938 but not selected. He played in 1500 games and was involved in 1,289 putouts.")[163]

(LF) **Ken Williams**: Williams was another one of those .300 plus hitters in the Browns' arsenal. He was difficult to contain to a single hit, but he already had more than 170 of them this 1922 season. Williams was deadly when there were runners on base and ranked as a slugger. (Williams would end a 14 season career in 1929 having played

---

[162] http://www.baseball-reference.com/players/t/tobinja01.shtml
[163] http://www.baseball-reference.com/players/f/fosteed02.shtml

for Cincinnati, St. Louis and Boston. He would appear at the plate 5,626 times in his career. He batted .319 career.)[164]

(CF) **Baby Doll Jacobson** Like Cy, William Chester Jacobson was an Illinois farm boy (Born Cable, Illinois August 16, 1890). He had traveled a path to the American League familiar to Cy; playing for the Rock Island Islanders in the Illinois-Indian-Iowa League (III) and then went on to the Southern Association, playing for Mobile, Chattanooga and Little Rock. He was a powerful man at 6-3 and 215 pounds. He played centerfield and had a strong throwing arm. The Browns took him from Detroit in 1915. He was out of the majors in 1916 but came back to them in 1917 and had been there ever since. He had batted .352 the previous year. (Jacobson appeared at the plate more than 6,000 times in 11 major league seasons. (1472 games) He had 1714 career hits and his lifetime batting average of .311 made him one of the top 100 hitters in the game.[165] He finished right behind Jackie Robinson. In1924 he had more outfield put-outs (488) than any other American Leaguer.)[166]

(2B): **Marty McManus**: McManus was a lean, mean baseball machine at 5-10, 160 pounds. He played only one year in the minors before coming to the majors. Born in Chicago in 1900, he made his inroads in the Texas League. He was now in his third year with the Browns. Like most of the other Browns, he was a .300 hitter. Only 22, he seemed to be a threat to opposing pitchers and seemed to have a bright future. (Indeed he did have a bright future. His career concluded after 15 seasons with a lifetime BA of .357 and nearly 9,000 trips to the plate. His home position was 2B but he also played 3B and shortstop. He was one of the top home run hitters of his day.)[167]

(C) **Josh Billings**: John Augustus "Josh" Billings was a player Cy knew something about. He had left the Louisville team the year before Cy got there. He also knew he had played on the Quincy, Illinois Gems in the III League in 1913. He had started his career with Cleveland

---

[164] http://www.baseball-reference.com/players/w/willike01.shtml
[165] http://www.baseball-reference.com/players/j/jacobba01.shtml
[166] http://www.baseball-reference.com/players/j/jacobba01.shtml
[167] http://www.baseball-reference.com/players/m/mcmanma01.shtml

and moved to the Browns for the 1919 season. He was one of the weaker hitters on the Browns team and only saw limited service as catcher. (In fact this was one of five games Billings would play in this season. He would head back to the minors in 1924 and spend another 14 seasons there.)[168]

(1B) **Pat Collins**: Collins was a rising star for the Browns. A Sweetwater, Missouri native, he was seeing a lot more action as catcher. He had come up through the tough Western League and was holding his own as a catcher and a hitter. He was a good long ball hitter and a misplaced pitch could spell disaster for an opposing team. He was also fleet of foot and could steal bases. (Collins spent ten seasons in the majors His lifetime BA was .254. He did make three appearances in World Series as a New York Yankee. In 1926 he was second on the AL Leader Board for bases stolen, but they came at a price. He was caught stealing 36 times, the fourth highest total in the league. Collins retired to the minors and little did Cy suspect that they would one day be teammates in the American Association League). [169]

(SS): **Wally "Spooks" Gerber** wasn't the strongest hitter on the Browns team but he seemed to be one of the most consistent. Born in Columbus, Ohio in 1914, he started his career with the Pirates in 1914 and stayed for 1915. He was picked up by the Browns in 1916 and worked his way into the starting lineup. Gerber was amazingly consistent and reliable. If he had a weakness it was an unusually high number of errors. He was usually an AL leader in errors at shortstop, but on the other hand he was also a leader in putouts. It was obvious he was a busy man on the Browns team. He batted .278 the previous year. (Gerber would end his ML career in 1929 and then play one more year in the American Association League for the Minneapolis Millers. In 1923 he finished fourth in the AL MVP race. He finished behind Babe Ruth, Eddie Collins and Harry Heilmann. He had a lifetime BA of .257)[170]

---

[168] http://www.baseball-reference.com/pl/player_search.cgi?search=Josh+Billings
[169] http://www.baseball-reference.com/players/c/collipa01.shtml
[170] http://www.baseball-reference.com/players/g/gerbewa01.shtml

(P): **Bill Bayne**: Cy knew that Bayne normally didn't start games, he finished them. He was a good relief pitcher. Bayne was also a pretty good hitter. In 1921 he had hit .300. (Bayne would end his 9-season career with a 31-32 record and a lifetime ERA of 4.84. and a lifetime BA of 3.30. He would go back to the Southern Association for several seasons of AA ball before retiring.)[171]

Cy went in and pitched the final innings of the game. He faced nine batters and walked two batters. He allowed one hit and made no errors but he could not save the game. The Browns won 7-6.

Next the Nationals went to Chicago's Comiskey Park to take on the Chicago White Sox. The games went like this:

**Friday, September 22, 1922:** White Sox 6 Washington 4. Pitching duties for the Nationals were handled by Tom Zachary. He gave up 11 hits in eight innings.

**Saturday, September 23, 1922:** White Sox 8 Washington 3. Walter Johnson gave up 11 hits but pitched the entire game.

**Sunday, September 24, 1922**: Washington 5 White Sox 4. Ray Francis pitched relief and saved the game for George Mogridge. Mogridge was now 17-13, the best won loss record on the team.

September 25, 26 and 27 were off days.

## Wednesday Septmber 28, 1922: SHIBE PARK, Philadelphia

Twenty nine year-old Ray Francis was having a tough rookie year when the Nationals rolled into Shibe Park in Philadelphia. He was a Texas pitcher who had limited success in the Texas Leagues (a very talented minor league team) and then moved to the Pacific Coast Leagues, another difficult league, where he played one marginal winning season (12-11) with the Washington Rainiers.

Now in St. Louis after a three-day layoff, the Nats were facing a hard series with the Athletics. It had started well. This was double-header day and the Nationals had won the first game 9-6 with George Mogridge going all nine innings. Eddie Rommel, a 25 game winner this season, absorbed the loss.

The second start fell to lefthander Francis. The Philly bats were ready for him and by the end of the second inning Francis allowed 10 Athletic

---

[171] http://www.baseball-reference.com/players/b/baynebi01.shtml

runs to score. It was decided by manager Milan to again give Cy the opportunity to pitch. Cy pitched 4.1 innings (finished the second and four more.) He allowed two more runs to score on three hits but committed no errors. The game ended 12-5 and Milan probably thought Cy did a respectable job in a tough situation. By the box scores we know he faced 17 batters, striking out three of them. Cy may have been thrilled to get into the game but starting ten runs in the hole was a serious deficiency. The lineup he was facing looked like this:

1. **Frank "Bugger" Welch,** (CF): Welch, born Birmingham, Alabama August 10, 1897, came to the Athletics courtesy of the Southern Atlantic and Virginia leagues where he had clearly excelled as a hitter. Thus far, he had proven no disappointment to the Phillies. While he was not yet a .300 hitter, he was getting close and hit .285 the previous season plus, he knocked in 45 runners. He was always a threat.[172] (Bugger would spend nine seasons in the bigs before retiring to the minors as a manager. His first stop would be to join the Atlanta Crackers (along with Ray Francis) and eventually become a manager of the Class C Beckley, West Virginia Black Knights in the Mid Atlantic League)[173]

2. **Frank Bruggy**,(C): An Elizabeth, New Jersey boy born in 1891, came up through the New England League (plus a partial season in the International League) had matured into a power hitter at Philly in his very first season, batting .310. He too was a multiple base threat when batting.[174] (Bruggy would spend five years in the majors and bat .277. He would not go back to the minors.)

3. **Tillie Walker** (LF): Walker was born in 1887 in Spartanburg, Tennessee and rose to power through the Carolina Association. He came to the majors in 1911. He was a workhorse and now had more than 5,000 plate appearances to his credit. The 1921 season was the only season he had batted better than .300 (.304) but he was always close. His worst season (1917) he batted. 246. He had great ability to "place" hits against the competition and this had made him a threat. (Tillie Walker would finish third in total bases on the leader boards in 1922. He would also go on to get 1,423 hits

---

[172] http://www.baseball-reference.com/players/w/welchfr01.shtml
[173] http://www.baseball-reference.com/minors/player.cgi?id=welch-001fra
[174] http://www.baseball-reference.com/players/b/bruggfr01.shtml

in his career He would return to the minors in to play five seasons of top minor league ball in the International League, Southern Association and "B" ball in the South Atlantic League[175])

4. **Joe Hauser** (1B): The Athletics were making the most out of this young rookie they found in the American Association. Born in Sheboygan, Wisconsin in 1899 he had burst onto the American League and was etching his names in the hearts of fans as a slugger-in-training. He was hitting above .300 this 1922 season. (Hauser would go ahead to bat above .300 in his first two ML seasons, but then his stardom would begin to fade. In 1927 he and Cy Warmoth would again team up in the minors. In 1922 and 1924 he would be rated one of the top ten sluggers in the American League, a league known for sluggers.)[176]

5. **Bing Miller** (RF). Miller came to the Athletics from his native Iowa where he played AA ball for the Clinton Pilots. Miller batted .288 his first season and hit nine home runs. He would improve in both categories this season. (When he finally left the majors in 1936 after 16 major league seasons, Bing Miller would be a household name. He would play in 18 World Series games, helping take two of those championships home to Philadelphia. He would twice be nominated to the Baseball Hall of Fame but not elected)[177]

6. **Chick Galloway** (SS): Born in Clinton, South Carolina August 4, 1896, Galloway came to the Phillies from the Southern Association where he had played for the Atlanta Crackers. in 1918 and 1919. This 1922 season was his best hitting year yet. He was hitting above .300. He also laid down a lot of sacrifice hits and that was something for Cy to be alert for. Galloway was all over the 1922 Leader Boards (Galloway played third and second as well as short stop. He would play 10 seasons in the majors, all of them for Philadelphia except the 1928 season when he played for Cleveland. He would not go back to the minors.[178])

7. **Jimmy Dykes** (3B): Jimmy Dykes was popular in Philly. He was born there Nov. 10, 1896. He played two years in the minors (one with the Blue Ridge League in 1917 and the other the Southern

---

[175] http://www.baseball-reference.com/players/w/walketi01.shtml
[176] http://www.baseball-reference.com/players/h/hausejo01.shtml
[177] http://www.baseball-reference.com/players/m/millebi02.shtml
[178] http://www.baseball-reference.com/players/g/galloch01.shtml

Association in 1919 where he played for Atlanta). What experience he didn't gain in the minors, he was getting in the majors. He played in 155 games the previous season. He seemed to be evolving into a perennial .300 hitter. He homered 16 times the previous year. He had finished 21st in Most Valuable Player polling. He was a threat hitting, fielding and running. (Jimmy Dykes would appear in 18 world series games. He would help return the World Series championships to Philadelphia in 1929 and 1930. The last seven seasons of his 22 ML seasons he would play for the Chicago White Sox. He would play in 2,282 games and have a lifetime batting average of .280. He would play in three World Series games and receive 11 nominations to the Baseball HOF. Unfortunately he would not be elected. He would move into major league management for five teams.)[179]

8. **Heine Scheer** (2B): Henry William Scheer was 21 when he came to Philadelphia to play. He played for Harvard in the Eastern League for just one season before getting the call up. So far he appeared to be far better at fielding than hitting. Cy would have judged him a .200 hitter at best. (Scheer lasted only two seasons in the majors. He would play AA Ball in Pennsylvania and Illinois before returning to the Eastern League. His career would end at age 38).[180]

9. **Slim Harriss** (P): William Jennings Bryan Harriss came to Philadelphia from the Texas League. He did not have a great won and lost record and often gave up home runs. (Harris would last nine seasons as a major league pitcher. His last 2.5 years he would spend with the Boston Red Sox. His ending record would be 95-135. He learned to not allow so many home runs and in 1923 led the league in home runs allowed per 9 innings pitched. He would go back to play AA ball for St. Paul, Milwaukee and Kansas City before making a three-game final appearance for Dallas in the Texas League in 1935)[181]

## Friday, September 29, 1922, Still in Philadelphia:

This was a "rubber" match in the Nationals final five game series with the Athletics for 1922. It turned out to be a thriller. The game was tied 2-2

---

[179] http://www.baseball-reference.com/minors/player.cgi?id=dykes-002jam
[180] http://www.baseball-reference.com/players/s/scheehe01.shtml
[181] http://www.baseball-reference.com/players/h/harrisl01.shtml

at the end of the 11th.inning. Nats' pitcher Eric Erickson was masterful and it looked like the Nationals would take the prize when Pete Lapan homered in the 12th. Unfortunately the Athletics had last bats and scored two runs. Score: Philadelphia 4 Washington 3. Eddie Rommel got the win and Erickson moved to 3-4.

It was one of Erickson's best showings of the year. He was now 4-12. (Unknown to Cy and Erickson, the pitcher was having his last year in the majors. He would end his major league career at 34-47 with a 3.85 ERA. He would play five games in the minors and the n disappear from baseball.)

Missing from the lineup with Washington was Philadelphia's George Sisler, the man many regarded as the perfect player. Sisler just this year had hit in 41 consecutive games, a record that would stand until broken by a player named Joe DiMaggio. Sisler suffered from a severe sinus condition that affected his eyesight and would make him miss the entire 1923 season. He hit .420 in 1922. He was elected to the Baseball Hall of Fame in 1939.

**Saturday, September 30, 1922, Game 1:** **Still in Philadelphia:** It was the final double header of the 1922 season for Washington. In game one Philly's Slim Harris and Tom Zachary faced off. It was a shutout until the fourth. The Nationals scored a run and the Athletics got two. Then in the fifth inning the Washington bats began to crack. They scored four runs. They added single runs in the sixth and seventh inning. The Athletics got one more in the eighth but it was not enough. After nine innings of pitching, Zachary got the win. He finished on 15-10 for the year. Final Score: Nationals 7, Athletics 3:

**Game 2:** In this game it was Francis taking on 31-year-old Eddie Rommel. Francis had things going his way until the fifth inning when he gave up four hits, including a homer by leftfielder Tillie Walker. Milan made no changes. The Phillies added two more runs and the game ended. Final Score: Athletics 7, Nationals 4. The win gave Rommel the pitching crown for the most wins in the season. He also won the category of most games pitched. He had pitched in 51 games.

It must have seemed to young Cy that his chances to prove himself in the majors was slipping away. The tired Washington pitchers seemed to have found a second wind. Perhaps they were being overly protective of their jobs. It was then he got the surprise of his life. He was to start against the New York Yankees in the final game of the year. This is the place where our story about Cy Warmoth began. His story was not conventional, but it was far from over.

**Sunday, October 2, 1922, Griffith Stadium Washington D.C.:** Wallace Warmoth won his first major league game. He struck out five batters, walked 5 and gave up five hits. The losing pitcher was Sad Sam Jones. Jones fell to 13-13 on the year. He pitched all nine innings and faced 38 batters. Warmoth batted 4 times, struck out only once. His previous BA of 1.000 fell to .286. His strike out victims included Babe Ruth. He pitched all nine innings.

# CHAPTER 11

# A Rookie Senator

## 1923

LIKE OPENING DAYS everywhere, the Washington Nationals began a new season with great hope. True fans of every team would let irrational hopes slip across their lips proclaiming "this could be *The Year*." It would not be *the year for* Cy Warmoth, nor would it be *the year* for the Nationals but little did Nationals fans suspect, nor could they get a clue from the disappointing season which awaited them in 1923, they *truly* were just one season away from Nirvana.

On the last day of the season of 1922, Cy truly glimpsed glory. He had single-handedly out-pitched Sad Sam Jones in a full nine-innings of baseball, striking out Babe Ruth in the process. From the point of personal satisfaction, this had to be like a gold miner finding a huge nugget after years of futile picking and digging. The win also earned him the call back, and probably (but have not been able to confirm this) an invitation to spring training in Tampa Florida. If he attended, he would have gotten to know a lot of the men he had only briefly met the season before. Spring training was a time of fun. Spring baseball came without so much pressure.

A major change had taken place in Washington baseball. The Nationals had a new player manager. Donie Bush, the often volatile and hard-nosed, long-time Detroit Tiger was now the skipper of the Washington Senators/Nationals. Milan was gone. Detroit placed Bush on the waiver list at the age of 33. He was quickly selected by Washington to replace "Deerfoot" as manager. Milan, a native of Linden, Tennessee, had written new records in the books with quick feet. In 1912 he stole 88 bases. His record was later broken by Ty Cobb. He stole 495 bases in sixteen seasons. Milan was moved to the Senator coaching staff as a token of appreciation for his many years of hard service.[182]

---

[182] http://en.wikipedia.org/wiki/Clyde_Milan

Bush, a native of South Bend, Indiana, was known for many things. For one thing he had spent years in the company of Ty Cobb. He was one of best shortstops ever produced in the dead ball era.[183] Cy had good success under the tutelage of Milan. Likely he wondered how this change would impact his fate in the major leagues. Bush was one of those guys who would kill *for you* if he liked you but would impale you on a sharp tongue if he didn't.

Rolling again into **Shibe Park, Wednesday April 18, 1923** to confront Connie Mack's Philadelphia Athletics would have been a little like Christians arriving at a Roman arena. Ceremonies varied from park to park. Had they opened in Washington, President Warren G. Harding might have thrown out the first pitch. Former President Howard Taft had started the tradition in Washington back in 1912. This same day New York governor Al Smith was throwing out the first pitch as New York Yankees unveiled their mammoth new stadium that would one day be called: "The House that Ruth Built." The attendance in Philadelphia this opening day was estimated at 20,000. More than 74,000 would attend the opener in New York.

Some major league baseball openers were more colorful than others. Most teams dressed in the hotels and paraded to the ball park. Some did it all the time since locker room facilities were less adequate than today. John McGraw, always the instigator, often made his New York Giants parade to the away ballparks when they were out of town.

The opening day games started a little later. Schools experienced massive absenteeism on opening days. Some cities countered the problem by starting school early on opening day and then dismissing early enough for the kids to go to the ball game.

The previous year had not been a particularly good one for "The Big Train" Walter Johnson. The man with the "disappearing fast ball" had finished 15-16. He had not been feeling well the previous season until April 18 (the sixth game) and then only got through five innings before calling for relief. This 1923 season he would duel with Slim Harriss in the season opener. He pitched the entire game but ended up the loser, 3-1

Cy Warmoth would not see action until April 23 when the Nationals strode into that still brand new Yankee Stadium I. It was a three-game series. In the first game of the series **Tuesday April 22, 1923** Walter Johnson became the first person to ever beat the Yankees in their palatial

---

[183] http://en.wikipedia.org/wiki/Donie_Bush

stadium when he eked out a 4-3 win, being relieved by Mogridge in the eighth inning. In their opening series the Yankees had won all four games from Boston.

**April 23, 1923 (Yankee Stadium):** Cy drew another start against the Yankees. This was his first effort with Bush as manager. Opposing Cy was Bullet Joe Bush. Bullet Joe had lost two very close games in the 1922 World Series against the New York Giants. The Giants had won the series 4-0-1 (tie). Cy showed no intimidation in this re-match with the fired up Yankees. He pitched all nine innings, held the Yankees to three hits and allowed only one run to score. The final score of the game was 2-1. Sam Rice and Goose Goslin scored the runs for Washington. Bob Meusel scored the only run for the Yankees, driven in by Aaron Ward. Babe Ruth, who went 0 for 3, and so was probably one of the runners walked (possibly an intentional walk ordered by Bush), paid Cy back for strikeout on their last meeting by stealing a base off him. Cy was off to a great start.[184] His professional record was now 2-0. He was 1-0 for the season.

**A BIT OF HISTORY:** While researching this game it suddenly occurred to the author that Cy might have been the first opposing pitcher to pitch a full nine innings against the Yankees in their new stadium and defeat them. Using information available online I was able to confirm that. The Yanks opened their season in a four-game stand at the new stadium. The Yankees swept all four games over the Boston Red Sox. While all four Yankee pitchers won their games, only two were able to pitch all nine innings. Bush and Bob Shawkey pitched a full nine innings. Carl Mays and Howard Ehmke needed relief. Cy added a milestone of sorts to his record by being **the first pitcher to pitch nine full innings and defeat the New York Yankees in their new stadium. He also became the second pitcher to defeat the Yankees in Yankee Stadium I.** The first was Walter Johnson. The second person to pitch nine innings and defeat the Yankees would be the Cleveland Indians' Eddie Rommel.

---

[184] http://www.baseball-reference.com/boxes/NYA/NYA192304230.shtml

## The Starting Line Up For the Game:

| Nationals | | | YANKEES | |
|---|---|---|---|---|
| Sam Rice | RF | 1 | *Whitey Witt+* | CF |
| Joe Evans | CF | 2 | *Joe Dugan++* | 3B |
| *Joe Judge*\* | 1B | 3 | **Babe Ruth** | RF |
| **Goose Goslin** | LF | 4 | Wally Pip | 1B |
| **Bucky Harris** | 2B | 5 | *Bob Meusel+++* | LF |
| Patsy Gharrity | C | 6 | *Wally Schang++++* | C |
| 7Roger Peckinpaugh | SS | 7 | *Aaron Ward+++++* | 2B |
| Bill Conroy | 3B | 8 | *Everett Scott++++++* | SS |
| Cy Warmoth | P | 9 | *BulletJoe Bush+++++++* | P |

**Bold Indicates Inducted Into Hall of Fame**

* \* Nominated to HOF 7 times
* + Led the AL in putouts as SS in 1916
* ++ 7 time nominee to HOF, never elected[185]
* +++ Played in 34 World Series games
* ++++ Played in 32 World Series games
* +++++ Played in 19 World Series games
* ++++++ Played in 27 World Series games
* +++++++ Bullet Joe pitched in 9 World Series games between 1912 and 1919

**Friday April 27, 1923:** Cy got another call to service against the Philadelphia Athletics at Griffith Stadium. The game started with legendary Walter Johnson on the mound against old timer Walt Kinney. Kinney was the first to get caught in an onslaught of hits and the Nationals scored four runs. A's manager Connie Mack jerked Kinney after the first out and sent in Eddie Rommel. Bush withdrew Johnson in the fourth and sent in Rubber Arm (Allen) Russell. Russell also had his problems, allowing 14 hits and six runs while only facing 11 batters. The score was then 9-9. Bush sent Cy into the game.

---

[185] http://www.baseball-reference.com/players/d/duganjo01.shtml

Rommel and Cy kept opposing batters at bay until the 12th inning when they each gave up another run. The game was called on account of either darkness or weather, probably the former. The scored ended up a 10-10 tie.

Cy pitched five innings, allowed 2 hits, walked 1 and allowed a run. It was another good outing for Cy but he neither added or detracted from his record. There was no winning or losing pitcher.[186]

**Monday April 30, 1923:** A few days later Cy got another chance to show his stuff. The Yankees were back in Washington to play four games. This time Bush pitted him against Sad Sam Jones. The Nationals gave Cy a comfortable 3-0 lead in the first inning. He did fair until the sixth inning when Bob Meusel popped a home run off him with nobody on base. Bush jerked him and sent in "Rubberarm" Russell. (Cy was charged with five of the six runs that scored in the sixth inning.) Russell pitched 1.2 innings and was charged with one run. He was relieved by newcomer Slim McGrew who gave up another nine runs. The final score was 17-4. Since the go ahead run belonged to Russell (who pitched less than two innings) he was charged with the loss. Cy batted twice and got thrown out and popped up. Now he was 1-1 on the season.

**Thursday May 3, 1923:** Cy also drew the chance to close the series. This time he took the mound opposite Herb Pennock, one of the top pitchers in the American League. Pennock, nicknamed the Knight of Kennett Square (Pennsylvania), started pitching in the America League at age 18 in 1912. He did not go to the minors until three years after his debut in the majors. He had pitched more than 20 games in the majors, winning most of them for Philadelphia. He pitched in his first World Series game at the ripe old age of 20. Boston picked him up and pitched him twice before "loaning" him to the AA International League. He emerged in the American League again in 1917 and seems to have disappeared from baseball in 1918, the year that world war shortened baseball. He came back to play for Boston in 1919. The New York Yankees purchased him from Boston in this year (1923) and he seemed to be a new force in pitching. (He would pitch 25 games this year and lose only six of them. He would be elected to the Baseball Hall of Fame in 1948. Pennock would pitch in 10 World Series games at the conclusion of five seasons while maintaining an average post-season ERA of 1.9. His lifetime record would be 241-162 (.598) and his lifetime ERA would be 3.60.

---

[186] http://www.baseball-reference.com/boxes/WS1/WS1192304270.shtml

During this contest, Cy pitched 6.2 innings before being pulled by Bush. It was a busy six innings. He was tagged for nine hits. He allowed three runs to score (2$^{nd}$, 4$^{th}$ and 7$^{th}$ innings,) the last run was the one that got him benched and caused the team to be defeated. Rubberarm Russell came back in and got a key strikeout. Bush sent in Jim Brillheart to finish the game. The Washington batters were not able to overcome the powerful pitching display of Pennock. Cy was charged with a hard-fought loss. He was now 1-2 on the year. In another touch of payback, Babe Ruth tagged Cy for a triple and walked twice. When the league leading Yankees left town they were in second spot, but the season was young and Washington was only six games (sixth in the league) behind the league leading Detroit Tigers.

**Tuesday May, 8 1923**: the Nationals were in Detroit for a game with the third place Tigers. Once again Cy was going to pitch in Navin Field. His rival pitcher was another man destined to have a long and great career in major league baseball. He was Sylvester "Syl" Johnson. Johnson pitched 10 games for Cleveland in 1922 and won seven of them. He was 1-1 when the Nationals came to town. There surely was underlying pressure in this game. It was the first meeting Donie Bush and his old (tor)mentor Ty Cobb.

Cy saw many familiar faces from his first trip to Tiger Town. New to the top of the order was (1) First Baseman **Luzerne "Lu" Blue,** the Maryland boy who attended Hall Military high school in Blairly, Maryland[187]. Ty Cobb and Bob Jones were still in the batting order of the year before.(2) Ducky Jones was on third[188]. (3)Ty Cobb, now 36, was still playing center field. (4) Bob Fothergill was now LF. (5) Harry "Slug" Heilmann, now a nine-season veteran and notorious slugger, was selected as right fielder. (6) Derrill "Del" Pratt, a recent acquisition from Boston who had hit .351 the previous year was set on second base. (8) Larry Woodall**,** a mere .344 hitter in 1922 would handle the catching duties. (9) Once again he would oppose Syl Johnson who had had finished 1922 with a 7-3 record in the prior season.

The first inning went well enough. The Nationals picked up a two-run pad when Goose Goslin homered with a runner (probably Judge) on base. In the third the Nationals added three more when Wade hit another off Johnson with two on. Cy stayed clean until the fourth when a run scored

---

[187] http://www.baseball-reference.com/players/b/bluelu01.shtml
[188] http://www.baseball-reference.com/players/j/jonesbo01.shtml

against him. He gave up another in the sixth. The box scores show his numbers as follows: 33 batters faced, struck out three, walked 7 and allowed seven hits. He committed only two errors. His teammates scored three more runs in the sixth. The game was called at the end of the seventh.

Cy's new teammate, Richard Frank "Rip" Wade had certainly lived up to his nickname. He was a product of the upper Midwest having been born in Duluth, Minnesota in 1898. He played A and AA ball in Minnesota before appearing in the Washington lineup. (After 25 games he would leave for the Southern Association from which Cy had come.) He would hit two home runs in those games, and Cy was the benefactor of this one.

Cy and his teammates should have won Brownie points from Bush. The victory was decisive and Cy pitched all seven innings of the game. Surely the outcome did not put a smile on the face of Cobb. Cy now had a 2-2 record for 1923 and his ERA was 2.0. He should have felt comfortable. The wily old fox Cobb struck out once walked once and hit into a putout. Cy had to feel his fortunes in Major League Baseball had improved. Now he had struck out both Ruth and Cobb. (Author's Note: In an appendix to the book "The Tiger Wore Spikes," by John Dennis McCallum there appears a chart showing how Ty Cobb fared against the pitchers he faced. This listing appears:

> Cobb vs. Warmuth (sic) 1 game 3 bats 1 hit. .333[189]. This record apparently did not include the game played against the Tigers in 1922. The possibility exists that Cobb was struck out more than once by Cy.)

The next day Tom Zachary put a feather in his own hat. He pitched a five-hitter in nine innings in a 4-1 victory to cap a two-day sweep of the Tigers.

**Sunday, May 13, 1923: Dunn Field, Cleveland Ohio.** Cy was destined to lose this game but in many ways it would be his most defining moment as a major league pitcher. Like Captain Kirk of the Starship Enterprise he was going where no one had gone before. He was about to do something that would write his name in the footnotes of baseball lore and legend. And, he probably didn't understand *exactly* what he had done until it was finished.

---

[189] The Tiger Wore Spikes, John McCallum, A.S. Burns and Company, New York p.p. 226

The Cleveland Indians had several remarkable players on their team. One of the least impressive, physically at least, was a young man by the name of **Joseph Wheeler "Joe" Sewell**. He was in some ways as remarkable as Babe Ruth. Sewell, only 5-6 and 155 pounds, was a shortstop and hitter extraordinaire. His career would span 14 seasons in the major leagues and by the time he retired, his ability to hit to base would be legend. Cy may not have known much about Sewell but he would have been aware of the pitching legend he found himself pitted against. His opposing pitcher, Stan Covelski, was one of those legendary pitchers who still had a legal right to throw the spitball. Covelski, a native of Shamokin, Pennsylvania, pitched in five games for the Philadelphia Athletics in 1912 then went to the Tri State League in Pennsylvania where he played until picked up by Cleveland at the age of 26. He had only two losing seasons in the major leagues. In 1923 he went 13-14. In 1924 his record was 15-16. (His career total would be 215-142 and his lifetime ERA 2.89.) While he *was* a mighty pitcher, he was blessed with teammates who excelled at hitting.) Here was the starting line ups for this special game.

| Nationals | | | Indians | |
|---|---|---|---|---|
| Ossie Bluege | 3B | 1 | Charlie Jamieson | LF |
| **Bucky Harris** | 2B | 2 | *Bill Wambsganass+* | 2B |
| Showboat Fisher | RF | 3 | **Tris Speaker** | CF |
| **Goose Goslin** | LF | 4 | Lou Guisto | 1B |
| Rip Wade | CF | 5 | Homer Summa | RF |
| Patsy Gharrity | C | 6 | **Joe Sewell** | SS |
| Roger Peckinbaugh | SS | 7 | Rube Lutzke | 3B |
| Bill Conroy | 1B | 8 | Glen Myatt | C |
| Cy Warmoth | P | 9 | **Stan Coveleski** | P |

**Bold Indicates Inducted Into Hall of Fame**

+*Bill Wambsganass made an unassisted triple play for the Indians in the 1920 World Series. It is still the only triple play in World Series history. Oct. 10, 1920 against the Dodgers while playing 2B he caught a line drive, stepped on a base and then tagged out a runner. There have been more perfect games pitched than unassisted triple plays.*[190]

---

[190] http://en.wikipedia.org/wiki/Unassisted_triple_play

In 1923 **Tris Speaker** was into his 17th major league season. (Born Tristram E. Speaker April 4, 1888 in Hubbard, Texas) He was already a legend in baseball in 1922. When he would finally retire in 1928 he would have played in 2,789 games and gone to the plate 11,988 times. He would amass 3,514 hits. As an outfielder, he also exhibited greatness and longevity. Speaker had a lifetime 6,935 putouts against 222 errors. He also had another 462 assists on his record. In later years his hair turned gray earning him the nickname The Gray Eagle. He played in 20 World Series games (1912, 1915, and 1920). He was the 1912 MVP for the American League. He is the only major league player to have three 20-game hitting streaks in the same season.

**Joseph Wheeler Sewell** (Born in 1898 in Titus, AL) played only one year in the minors. He had played for the New Orleans Pelicans of the Southern Association in 1920. Cy had never faced Sewell before this day. He was a phenomenon. The late L. Robert "Bob" Davids wrote an illuminating piece about Sewell. Davids founded the Society for Baseball Research. In his article he noted that Sewell was a very rare performer in professional baseball.

"In spite of these ups and downs, there were two players who stood out in their respective eras. They were Joe Sewell in the period 1920-33, when there were fewest strikeouts, and Nellie Fox, 1947-65, who played in an era of increasing numbers. Fox led his league 11 times while Sewell held the title 9 times. While Sewell's yearly totals were about half those of Fox, the two were nearly comparable for their eras.

"On the pitcher analysis, we find that Sewell, who batted left handed, was fanned by southpaws 44 times and right-handers 69 times. On two occasions he was fanned twice in the same game. **The first time was on May 13, 1923, when Wally (Cy) Warmoth, a rookie southpaw (of the Nationals), set him down both times. The next time was May 26, 1930, and Lefty Pat Caraway of the White Sox did it twice that time . . . .**

"In his 14 years of play, Sewell was never fanned by any pitcher more than 4 times. Nine different pitchers accomplished that. They included the aforementioned Blaeholder (George alleged inventor of the slider), Bob Shawkey, Walter Johnson, Urban Shocker, Waite Hoyt, and Earl Whitehill, all long-service hurlers, and three short-time lefties, Bill Bayne, Mike Cvengros, and Ed Wells. Yet, Sewell says it was none of these who gave him the most trouble. "The hardest pitcher for me was Hubert 'Dutch' Leonard of Detroit. He was a left-hand spitball pitcher, and he was mean with it."[191]

Sewell went to bat 8,321 times and struck out only 113 times. It is little wonder he ended up in the Hall of Fame, inducted in 1977.[192]

Cy started the game against the Indians and pitched seven innings, replaced in the eighth and final inning by Jim Brillheart. Cy struck out four batters. We know two of those strikeouts were against Sewell. Cy struck out two other batters and Brillheart struck out one. The other players who struck out in the game were Jamieson, Guisto and Tris Speaker.

**Possible Moment of History**: *If Cy struck Tris Speaker out, it would mean that he struck out three of the very first six inductees into the Baseball Hall of Fame.*

Speaker had two hits and two RBI's. Both of the batters in the line up ahead of him (Wambsganss and Jamieson) scored. Myatt, Coveleski and Sewell also scored. The Nationals actually out hit the Indians 10-7. The Nationals had two double plays, yet they still lost the game 5-2. Cy batted once and struck out. A pinch hitter was used the rest of the way. Cy's record on the season was now 2-3.[193]

Cy's Nationals' team had a different face on it. George "Showboat" Fisher was in right field. This was his first year playing for the Nationals. (*He was a good hitter but would only last four seasons in the majors. His lifetime BA would be .335. He would return to the minors and play more than a 1,000 games.*)

**Thursday May 17, 1923: Comiskey Park I, Chicago**—Cy's next stop on his rookie voyage would be Chicago. The White Sox still struggled following the cheating scandal that erupted there in 1919-1920. (Discussed in Chapter 7) Rightly or wrongly, much of the blame was placed at the feet of miserly Charlie Comiskey. Whatever the truth may be, no one could deny that Comiskey had started a baseball tradition and empire that still thrives today. The Chicago White Sox won their first World Championship in 1906 defeating the Chicago Cubs. In 1917 the

---

[191] http://research.sabr.org/journals/sewell-was-a-real-fox
[192] http://www.baseball-reference.com/players/s/seweljo01.shtml
[193] http://www.baseball-reference.com/boxes/CLE/CLE192305130.shtml

White Sox defeated the New York Giants 4-2. The next was the infamous series in 1919 when the White Sox lost to the Cincinnati Red Sox. The scandal-tainted series was scheduled to go nine games but ended in eight. In 1959 the Sox made it back to the World Series but lost to the Los Angeles Dodgers 4 games to 2.

The White Sox would not go back to World Series play until 2005 when they defeated the Houston Astros in a four-game sweep.

The 1919 Series had not only jeopardized the team, it nearly wrecked professional baseball. The lineup for the game looked like this:

| Nationals | | | White Sox | |
|---|---|---|---|---|
| 1 Ossie Bluege | 3B | 1. | *Harry Hooper+* | RF |
| 2 **Bucky Harris** | 2B | 2, | Harvey McClellan | SS |
| 3 Showboat Fisher | RF | 3. | **Eddie Collins** | 2B |
| 4 **Goose Goslin** | LF | 4. | *Earl Sheely++* | 1B |
| 5 Joe Evans* | CF | 5 | Johnny Mostill | CF |
| 6 *Muddy Ruel*** | C | 6. | Willie Kamm | 3B |
| 7 Roger Peckinbaugh | SS | 7. | Roy Elsh | LF |
| 8 Bill Conroy | 1B | 8. | **Ray Schalk** | C |
| 9 Cy Warmoth | P | 9 | Sloppy Thurston | P |

**HALL OF FAMERS NAME IN BOLD**

\* Evans, born Meridian Mississippi 1895, played 11 seasons in the majors. He had played seven seasons for Cleveland before joining the Nationals. Lifetime BA was .259

\*\* Nominated to Hall of Fame 10 times but never elected, still consider a legendary player of the era.

+ Harry Hooper: 17 ML seasons, mostly for Boston. Six—time nominee to Hall of Fame, never elected

++ Sheely finished 2$^{nd}$ in MVP for American League in 1926

As Cy looked over the lineup he had to be most awed by the presence of **Eddie Collins**. Collins' career spanned 18 seasons at the time of this game. A formidable infielder and batter, Collins had been striking fear into the hearts of pitchers since arriving in the majors in 1906. He was a member of the 1919 Black Sox team but was not tainted by scandal. He had already played in 34 World Series games. He played four World Series games for the Philadelphia Athletics and two for the White Sox. *(He would spend 22 seasons in the majors, retiring in 1930. He went to the plate an astounding 12,037 times and had a lifetime BA of .333. He was elected to the Hall of Fame in 1939.)*

The top of the order was worrisome. Four of the top five in the order hit .300 or better in 1922. McClellan was the exception. His first two years in the big show he batted .333. The previous year he batted only .226. Kamm was also a rookie but had been hitting well. Elsh, a rookie at age 32, had never played in minors and was pretty much a mystery man. Schalk, a veteran of 12 seasons, had never batted less than .300 with a high of .379 in 1922. *(Schalk would conclude his fantastic career in 1929. He caught 1,762 games. He was nominated to the HOF 17 times before being elected in 1955.)* Thurston was also a rookie and had pitched only 14 games. He had played minor league ball in the Pacific Coast Leagues.)

The game would go ten innings and Cy would pitch to 43 of 44 batters. He would give up 12 hits with Hooper hitting him three times. Kamm and Mostill nailed him twice each. Collins, Sheely, Elsh and Schalk hit Cy once each. The other hit was snagged by old timer Amos Strunk, pinch hitting for Schalk. Strunk came into major league baseball in 1908. Cy struck out none of the batters he faced and his teammates did the put outs. Oddly, for Cy, he tagged the opposing pitcher for a double, his only hit of the game. His BA was now .176.

To salvage the game Manager Bush sent in the "Big Train" Walter Johnson to face the last batter. Cy was victorious after ten innings and his record improved to 3-3 on the season.

The next day the Washington Post Headline read:

**Long Drives in Tenth Puts Warmoth Across:** The subhead read: **Southpaw Wobbles Badly and Johnston is Put in When Enemy Makes Last Stand—Fisher. Goslin and Evans Produce Punch.**

**<u>Monday, May 21, 1923 Sportsman Park III</u>:** The train steamed back into St. Louis for a three-game series. Cy should not have felt like a stranger here as he saw the green farm meadows of Southern Illinois roll by. Tom Zachary was the opening pitcher for game one. The Browns' bats exploded. Zachary gave up 5 runs in the first four innings. Allen Russell came in for five innings and gave up two hits but no runs. Mogridge pitched to 8 batters and Johnson faced one. The final score was 9-8 and Johnson was charged as the losing pitcher.

The Browns, like the Nationals, were not off to a fast start. The Browns were now in sixth place in the American League. The Nationals were one game ahead of them and the White Sox were a game behind them. The Yankees were leading the league and Philadelphia trailed the Yankees four games. Cleveland and Detroit were two and two-and-a-half games behind respectively. There was a lot of pressure from the owners to improve the records. Remember in 1923 the only way the clubs had to make money was by fans paying to get into the games. Losing teams attracted fewer spectators. Cy faced pretty much the same team he had faced in 1922.

| Nationals | | | BROWNS | |
|---|---|---|---|---|
| Ossie Bluege | 3B | 1 | Jack Tobin | RF |
| **Bucky Harris** | 2B | 2 | Wally Gerber | SS |
| **Sam Rice** | RF | 3 | Baby Doll Jacobson | CF |
| Joe Judge | 1B | 4 | Ken Williams | LF |
| Rip Wade | LF | 5 | Marty McManus | 2B |
| Joe Evans | C | 6 | Pat Collins | C |
| Roger Peckinbaugh | SS | 7 | Gene Robertson | 3B |
| *Patsy Gharrity* | C | 8 | Dutch Schliebner | 1B |
| Cy Warmoth | P | 9 | Elam Vangilder | P |

## HALL OF FAMERS NAME IN BOLD

This ballgame featured two pitchers, both of whom may have played some of the same teams in the minors, squaring off on the mound in Sportsman's Park. This day Cy faced Elam Van Gilder, a native of Cape Girardeau, Missouri, who had played in the Triple I league in 1917. He also pitched some games in the Western League. Vangilder got called up by the St. Louis Browns in 1919 and he had done well, finally having a positive W-L record in 1922 when he won 19 games and lost 13. He also scored four saves. Vangilder was big for a pitcher of his day, standing 6-1 and weighing 190 pounds.[194]

---

[194] http://www.baseball-reference.com/players/v/vangie01.shtml

The lineup was almost the same as when he faced the Browns the previous September. Eddie Collins had shifted from catcher to first base. Gene Robertson was a new face. He had batted .296 in 1922. He had replaced Foster at third base. Of course Van Gilder was a new challenger. In the previous contest Cy had faced Bill Payne.

The game went well the first inning. Neither team scored. In the second inning two Browns scored when Cy's opposing pitcher hit a home run off Cy with one runner on base. Washington scored once. Cy struck out three batters and his team was able to get put outs on the others. The Nationals allowed no more runs to score while scoring two of their own. The final scores of the game was 3-2. Cy now owned a lifetime 5-3 record.[195] His record of the year improved to 4-3. He went to the plate four times, striking out once, hitting once and was put out twice. His only hit was a triple. His BA was .190.

**Sunday May 27, 1923:** Cy and the Nats returned to Washington to face the Yankees again on Sunday May 27, 1923. Griffith Stadium was the largest of all wooden structure of its kind in 1923. A cluster of 6,000 fans, many of them women and school kids, turned out for the event. Perhaps some came to see the new pitcher, Wally Warmoth (Washington newspapers called him Wally) the man that had set down Joe Sewell twice, struck out Babe Ruth and Ty Cobb (and maybe Tris Speaker) go head to head again with Bullet Joe Bush. Cy was actually becoming known in Washington. The Nationals even paraded him off in uniform to a Canadian game. Yet the stadium was less than half full and that said loads about the year the Nats were having.

It was not to be a glorious homecoming for the homespun pitcher from Illinois. In some ways it would be the beginning of the end. Something was happening to Cy and there are no records to explain. It could be any of the things that causes pitchers to blow up. No doubt he had performed as well as most of the other Nationals pitchers. Even Johnson was having a tough year.

Cy was not getting a lot of batters called out on strikes but neither was he being hammered. He had given up only two home runs thus far in his career. Most of the batters were hitting into putouts. If there was anything wrong with his pitching, it was probably his percentage of batters walked. He had been fortunate to this point because the usually lethargic

---

[195] http://www.baseball-reference.com/boxes/SLA/SLA192305210.shtml

Washington hitting machine had hit well when he was pitching. Surely Bush and Ban Johnson had been getting nervous over this pitcher from nowhere. Perhaps they were searching for another Walter Johnson. They may have feared their Big Train was getting low on coal and steam. When he was good, he was very, very, good but there were not so good days. Bush was known to favor pitchers who could pitch an entire game. Yet Bush was quick to jerk pitchers from the mound.

Truth be known, the opponents were probably learning to read him. His lefty style was less of a puzzle than the day he showed up and struck out the great Babe Ruth. Ruth had yet to homer on him, and not many pitchers that faced "The Great Bambino" could say that. Ruth was known to jaw hard at those pitching to him.

The Yankees came at Cy with full force. He must have been like a pesky gnat to them. They brought exactly the same lineup he had faced earlier this season. The Yankees came to Washington in easy control of the American League. The Yankees had won 24 and lost 10. They were four games ahead of the Philadelphia Athletics and six games ahead of Cleveland. Washington was in fifth spot, 8-1/2 games behind the Yanks.[196]

Young Wally (Cy) got in trouble in the very first inning when the sly Long Bob Meusel connected for a home run with two on and two out.[197] The 6-3 190-pound Yankee stallion slammed 16 homers in 1922.[198]

Cy gave up another run in the third inning. No more runs, but he walked seven batters in the first five and one-third innings. Apparently he had several runners on base in the start of the sixth inning. Bush replaced him with a 26-year-old right handed pitcher named John "Bonnie" Hollingsworth they had acquired from Pittsburgh. Hollingsworth finished nine games for the Pirates in 1922. His total major league experience measured 13.2 innings.

Hollingsworth also had a tough time but the game ended 8-1. Hollingsworth was still not able to get a save. Cy could certainly empathize with his reliever; he had walked into several such situations since becoming a Senator. Cy's record was now 4-4 on the season.

The Yankees probably felt some accomplished revenge against the pesky Cy. No one would have enjoyed it more than Miller "Mighty Mite" Huggins, the coach who did not give him a second chance when they were

---

[196] http://www.baseball-reference.com/games/standings.cgi?date=1923-05-26
[197] http://www.retrosheet.org/boxesetc/1923/B05270WS11923.htm
[198] http://www.baseball-reference.com/boxes/WS1/WS1192305270.shtml

playing for the St. Louis Cardinals in 1916. Huggins was now finding fame and some fortune managing the New York Yankees.[199]

There was no game on Monday May 28, 1923. The Yankees had a day off in D.C. On Tuesday afternoon the series resumed.

**Game 2 Tuesday May 29, 1923:** A smaller crowd of about 3,500 was present. The guardians of the mounds were Waite "Schoolboy" Hoyt for the Yankees and Tom Zachary for the Nationals. Hoyt earned his nickname from his early start in the majors. The New York Giants through the wisdom of John McGraw signed him as a free agent in 1918 and farmed him out. He started pitching in the minors at the ripe old age of 15 and by the time the Giants signed him he had played for several minor league teams in the Eastern League, the Southern Association and the International League. From his unusual start he was dubbed "The Schoolboy Wonder."[200] His debut in the majors came, according to Baseball-Reference.com, on July 24, 1918 at age 18. The records on the New York Giants from that period are scant. His later records are not hidden. He lasted 21 seasons in the majors, playing for the Giants, Red Sox, Yankees, Tigers, Athletics, Dodgers, and Pirates. His most productive years were with the Yankees from 1921-1929. His win-loss record was 237-182. In the Yankee uniform he won 157 of those games. He became the best of the Yankee players in their early 20th Century golden era. He was elected to the Hall of Fame in 1969.[201]

Zachary was no pushover. He had winning seasons in 1921, 1922 and 1924. His other six seasons with the Nationals he had a losing record. He would end his career at 186-191. The Yankee bats knocked Zachary out in the first inning. The final score was 4-2 with Allen Russell pitching seven of the nine innings.[202]

**Game 3 Wednesday May 30, 1923:** was the first of a double header. Walter Johnson was on the mound for the Nationals. Herb Pennock (another Yankee pitcher bound for the Hall of Fame got the Yankee call). Pennock stayed on the mound for all nine innings. Walter Johnson, the best Nationals pitcher ever, and maybe the best pitcher in the history of

---

199  http://www.baseball-reference.com/boxes/WS1/WS1192305270.shtml
200  http://en.wikipedia.org/wiki/Waite_Hoyt
201  http://www.baseball-reference.com/players/h/hoytwa01.shtml
202  http://www.baseball-reference.com/boxes/WS1/WS1192305290.shtml

baseball, lasted only one inning. It took five more Nationals pitchers to get through the game. The final score of game three was 6-4.[203]

**Game 4 Wednesday May 30, 1923**: In short, the Yankees had decimated the Washington pitching staff in the three previous games. Game two of the double header brought back Bullet Joe Bush, who had pitched all nine innings of the game against Cy. George Mogridge who was also off to a weak start in the 1923 season had been reserved for the start of this game. The Yankee batters were held at bay for two innings. The good start came to a wood-thumping halt early in the third inning when Babe Ruth knocked one over the wall with two men on base. Cy was sent in to finish up the inning. It was a brief appearance. He faced four batters, giving up one hit and walking one. Two runs scored. The score was 5-2 when he left the game. Bush sent Paul Zahniser in to finish the game. He gave up another four runs. The Yankees won 9-5. It is interesting to note that Bullet Joe gave Cy something else to remember him by. He hit him with a pitch on one of his two trips to the plate. It is hard to imagine that being hit by a pitch thrown by a guy nicknamed Bullet Joe did not hurt. Looking at the stats it appears that Cy did not appear at the plate but when the Retrosheet of the same game reveals Cy and Mogridge (both Senator pitchers) were hit by pitched balls. On the Yankees side it seems that Babe Ruth was hit twice and short stop Lewis Scott had also twice been hit by pitched balls. One has to wonder if a game of bean ball had begun. (Ruth hit a home run off Mogridge in the third.)[204]

**June 2, 1923 Griffith Park, Washington D.C.** The Philadelphia Athletics came back to town and Cy drew opening honors on a double header day. The Senators bats cracked early and the team scored two in the first and third innings. They added another in the fourth but the A's got hot in the 4th and 5th innings scoring a total of six runs. Cy pitched 8 innings, being relieved by Jim Brillheart in the 9th. Cy pitched a solid game but allowed six runs on seven hits. Brillheart gave up a homer in the ninth. The A's won 7-5. Cy was now 4-5 on the season.

What had begun as a marvelous experience for Cy was beginning to look more like a nightmare. Pitching on the Washington team was lousy and the fans and sportswriters let the owners and managers know about it.

---

[203] http://www.baseball-reference.com/boxes/WS1/WS1192305301.shtml
[204] http://www.baseball-reference.com/boxes/WS1/WS1192305302.shtml

Attendance was down and that affected beer and hot dog sales. The final score of baseball was always measured in profit

Suddenly it was Tiger time in the nation's capitol.

The Tigers came back to D.C. Tuesday June 5 for a three-day series. Nationals Hurler Tom Zachary went to the mound to try and regroup the team from the thrashing by the Yankees. It was a visit in vain. Zachary lasted only until the fifth inning when Bush waved him to the dugout with runners on base and the score 1-0, Detroit ahead. Bush replaced Zachary with Allen Russell who did an impressive job. He faced 18 batters, allowed one hit, gave up two hits and struck out one. Still two of the runners already on base when he arrived at the mound scored and the game was lost 3-0. Zachary's W-L was now 4-5.[205]

On Wednesday, June 6, 1923, The Big Train Walter Johnson pulled into Griffith Park. He faced Ray Francis who just the year before had been a Nationals pitcher, leaving with a 7-18 record. If Francis had learned any new tricks for the Tigers they did not reveal themselves. The Nationals pummeled their old teammate with 12 hits including a double and a triple. Washington won 5-1.[206]

**Thursday June 7, Griffith Stadium Washington, D.C:**

The series was tied and it fell to Cy Warmoth to break the tie. The only player on the team he had not faced before was the pitcher, Herman "Old Folks" Pillette. Pillette was in his fourth season in the majors and his third with Detroit. He came from the Pacific Coast League (minor). Pillette's first year at Cincinnati he pitched only one inning. The previous season he went 19-12 for the Tigers.[207]

The Detroit line up looked like this:

**Detroit Tigers**

| | | |
|---|---|---|
| 1 | Fred Haney | 3B |
| 2 | Lu Blue | 1B |
| 3 | Ty Cobb | CF |
| 4 | Bob Fothergill | LF |

---

[205] http://www.baseball-reference.com/boxes/WS1/WS1192306050.shtml
[206] http://www.baseball-reference.com/boxes/WS1/WS1192306060.shtml
[207] http://www.baseball-reference.com/players/p/pillehe01.shtml

**Detroit Tigers**

| | | |
|---|---|---|
| 5 | Harry Heilmann | RF |
| 6 | George Cutshaw | 2B |
| 7 | Topper Rigney | SS |
| 8 | Johnny Bassler | C |
| 9 | Herman Pillette | P |

The game began with both sides scoring. The Tigers took two runs in the first inning. Cy was saved when his teammates came up and scored three of their own in the bottom of the inning. In the second inning the Tigers scored another but Washington could not score. The game was tied 3-3. No Detroit runs scored in the third and when the Nationals came to bat they exploded for five runs. Bush sidelined Cy and sent in Allen Russell. Rubber Arm subdued the Tigers allowing only 3 hits and not allowing a score. In the meantime the Senators exploded again racking up eight more runs. The game was won 16-4 and Cy was given credit for the win. Cy was now 5-5 on the year. *(Author's Note: The records are unclear where this fourth run came from. If it did not score in the third it had to score in the fourth, so Cy may have opened pitching the fourth inning before Bush jerked him.)*

**Saturday, June 9, 1923:** [208]

Two days later the St. Louis Browns were in town for a three-game series. This game was to be a shootout between Paul Zahniser and the legendary Urban Schocker. It was a close match. The Washington Nationals knocked in two runs in the first inning. The Browns scored a run in the second. The third inning was scoreless. In the fourth the Browns bats barked loudly and five runs scored. Bush removed Zahniser and sent in Jim Brillheart. Brillheart did well by allowing no more runs and striking out two batters while walking one. Bush sent Cy in to pitch to the finish. Facing three batters, he struck out one and let the other two hit into put-outs. The game ended 5-4. Zahniser took the loss and Shocker who pitched all nine innings for the Browns recorded his eighth win.

**Friday, June 15, 1923:** [209] The next challenge would come from the Chicago White Sox at Griffith Stadium. The Sox were seven games out

---

[208] http://www.baseball-reference.com/boxes/WS1/WS1192306090.shtml
[209] http://www.baseball-reference.com/games/standings.cgi?date=1923-06-15

of the basement. The Nationals, miracles of miracles, had risen to fourth in the league. The basement was firmly occupied by the Boston Red Sox, some 37 games out of the lead. The American League leading Yankees had lost fewer games (54) than the Red Sox had won (61).

The first game on June 14 pitted Tom Zachary against Sloppy Thurston. Thurston won the game easily. The first six Sox batters sent Zachary to the bench. He was replaced by Allen Russell who controlled the game through another six innings before getting in trouble. Zahniser and Hollingsworth each pitched an inning. The final score was 7-3. Russell took the loss and moved his record to 0 and 4.

The lineup on June 15 had Cy scheduled to start. The Sox lineup was nearly identical to the one Cy had faced in Comiskey Park. The only one new to Cy was the pitcher, Charlie Robertson. Robertson, a Texas native, had pitched mostly in the American Association before coming to Chicago. He pitched two innings in 1919 and then went back to the minors to pitch for the Minneapolis Millers until being called up again by the White Sox in 1922. He had finished 1922 with a 14-15 record.[210]

The game stayed scoreless until the third when Cy let a run score. Bush sidelined Cy in the seventh. He allowed five runs on five hits, walked four and was charged with five errors. He scored no strikeouts. The Big Train came in to relieve him and allowed three hits and one home run. Bibb Falk, a pinch hitter, hit the home run. The final score was 8-6. Cy got the win and Johnson scored a save. Cy's record was now 6-5. The Nationals were now only 10 games behind the Yankees.

At this point in the season Cy, and some of it was sheer luck, actually had the best pitching record on the Nationals team. Johnson was 6-5.; Russell was 0-4, Zachary was 5-5, Zahniser was 1-1, and Bonnie Hollingsworth was 3-5. George Mogridge, 1-2, had been inactive since May 26. Cy was certainly holding his own. However a pattern was emerging, Cy was getting into trouble and other pitchers were winning his games for him. This likely was creating tension in the bullpen. Cy needed his mastery back.

**Tuesday, June 19, 1923:** The Nationals were hosting a lot of home games, and now the Cleveland Indians were back at Griffith Stadium. The top five of the order was a tough one, but one he had faced before: Charlie Jamieson, Bill Wambsgnass, Tris Speaker, Lou Guisto and Joe Connolly. Cy faced these five and struck one of them out. Of those five batters Jamieson and Connolly struck out. We are unsure which one was Cy's conquest. He

---

[210] http://www.baseball-reference.com/players/r/roberch01.shtml

walked three batters. Perhaps Bush took Cy out of the game while a batter was at the plate, but he jerked him.

What followed was almost unbelievable. Bush benched Cy after hitting LF Charlie Jamieson with a bad pitch. Cy was followed by Tom Zachary. Zachary faced 22 batters in four innings. He gave up two home runs, four hits, walked three other batters and was charged with four errors. Five runs scored while Zachary was on the mound. Bush next sent in Jim Brillheart to pitch. Brillheart walked three batters, struck one out and allowed no scores. He faced only seven batters. The tour was finished out by Allen Russell who also faced seven batters in two innings. Russell gave up one home run. The game ended and somehow, remarkably, the Nationals won.

It seems the Indians pitching staff was also having problems. Sherrod "Sherry" Smith allowed five runs to score in five and two-thirds innings, all of six hits with no home runs being hit. George Uhle pitched three batters and then turned the game over to James Edwards to close. The Nationals went ahead on Edwards by scoring two more runs. It was nine innings of total confusion. The final score was 7-6 and Russell picked up his first win of the year. Not all the pitching gifts had Cy's name on them.

**Friday, June 22, 1923**: [211] The Nationals had another good chance to improve their league standings when they arrived at Shibe Park in Philadelphia for a five-game series with the Athletics. The A's were in second and only five-and-one-half games short of pulling even with the Yankees. They were at home and meant business. Washington was in sixth place but only five games behind the A's. The Nationals could, by the magic of mathematics, shoot up the league ladder. So, both teams were hungry.

The Big Train moved the Nationals up a notch in the first game on Friday the 22nd. Johnson and Slim Harriss went toe-to-toe for nine innings. Johnson had a six-hitter and Harriss an eight hitter. The Nationals won 3-2.

On Saturday, June 23[212] the hopes for a five-game sweep died an ugly death. The Athletics knocked starting pitcher Allen Russell out of the game in the third inning, scoring six runs. Paul Zahniser stepped in and gave up another four runs. The Nationals lost 10-5. Rookie Rube Walberg[213], another baseball legend in the making, got the win for the Athletics, thanks

---

[211] http://www.baseball-reference.com/boxes/PHA/PHA192306220.shtml
[212] http://www.baseball-reference.com/boxes/PHA/PHA192306230.shtml
[213] http://www.baseball-reference.com/players/w/walberu01.shtml

to a save by Eddie Rommel. Walberg would be a 155-game winner by the time he retired in 1937. Rommel would win 171 games in his 13-season career which would end in 1932. He is often remembered for the fact that he pitched 17 home run balls to Babe Ruth, more than any other pitcher.

Whatever ailed George Mogridge apparently healed by the next day June 24[214]. He came out and pitched a sold nine-innings, also allowing only six hits. Bob Hasty, a pitcher the A's found in the good old Southern Association, retired in the sixth and Curly Ogden, another Pennsylvania pitcher, tried to rescue him. (Ogden would later play in a World Series as a National.) Ogden's efforts were not fruitful. The Nationals won 8-0. Roger Peckinpaugh and Bucky Harris hit homers for the Nationals. Mogridge improved his record 2-4. The Nationals led the series 2-1.

There were now two games remaining in a critical series. Cy is not scheduled to start either game. He had (until this series) the best pitching record on the pitching staff for this season. It is necessary to wonder why Cy is not getting a start. Could it be due to an injury? Has he fallen out of favor with temperamental Donie Bush? Something seems to be out of square.

Game Four takes place on Monday June 25, 1923[215]. Bonnie Hollingsworth gets the starting call from Manager Donie Bush. It is another smoker. Eddie Rommel of the Athletics will last the full nine innings. It will take three Nationals pitchers to last eight innings. Hollingsworth allowed only two hits but walked five of the 12 batters he faced. Allen Russell replaced him. He stayed three innings and only allowed three hits and a single run to score. Bush sent him to the bench in favor of Tom Zachary. Zachary pitched nearly flawless baseball but the game went to the Athletics 3-0. Now the A's were up by three.

Finally at Shibe it is Tuesday, June 26[216] and Walter Johnson gets his second start in five days. He lasts four innings. He has given up seven runs on 10 hits while striking out one batter. The score is 6-5. Zahniser replaces Johnson for one inning. He faces eight batters, gives up three hits, walks one but four runs score. At the end of five innings the score is 6-1, Nationals trailing. Bush sends Cy into the game. He stays two innings. Five runs score on five hits, yet no home runs were hit. He walks two batters and fans two batters. When he leaves the game score is 16-7. The

---

[214] http://www.baseball-reference.com/boxes/WS1/WS1192306240.shtml
[215] http://www.baseball-reference.com/boxes/PHA/PHA192306250.shtml
[216] http://www.baseball-reference.com/boxes/PHA/PHA192306260.shtml

game is finished by another Nashville Volunteers recruit from the Southern Association. His name is Skipper Friday.[217] Friday throws right. This is the only year he will appear in the majors. He will pitch 30 innings and earn two saves. His record will be 0-1. There was no save on this disastrous day. Final score is 16-7. Now the series is decided 3-2 the Athletics triumphed at home.

The Nationals go to Boston and evenly split a four game series. They have slipped to seventh in the league and their pitching is the talk of the town in Washington D.C. Some say the pitchers, including the beloved Walter Johnson, are washed up. Others say Donie Bush is doing a lousy job utilizing his pitching staff, complaining that he is too quick to change pitchers in a game. July arrives with a major opportunity. The Nationals are going to Yankee Stadium for a four-game series with the Yankees. The series will conclude on Independence Day with a double-header.

**Game 1: Monday, July 2 Yankee Stadium[218]:** Bush chooses Tom Zachary to lead off in the series. He will pitch opposite Bob Shawkey, a 32-year-old right hander who has been pitching for the Yankees since 1915. He has won 20-games or more four different times since becoming a Yankee. In 1920 his ERA of .245 was the lowest in the American League. There are no surprises in the lineup. Fred Hoffman will catch. The Yankees greet their 10,000 fans with a barrage of hits. Ruth homers off Zachary in the first inning with two on. Pipp homers in the second off Skipper Friday. By the end of the third nine Yankee runs have scored. Hollingsworth closes the game, allowing no runs. The final score is 13-1.

Game 2: July 3 Yankee Stadium 1:[219] George Mogridge finally silences the Yankee bats. In a 15-inning thriller, Bullet Joe Bush and Mogridge and their teams engage in baseball chess mastery. Mogridge gives up 12 hits. Bullet Joe gives up eight. The game is scoreless until the eighth when Bullet Joe hit a homer off Mogridge. No runs scored again until the 15th inning when Babe Ruth sailed one into the stand to win the game for the Yankees. Final score: 2-1.

Game 3: July 4 Yankee Stadium 1: Game 1 of a Double Header:[220] Attendance was huge. By the start of the second game it was estimated

---

[217] http://www.baseball-reference.com/players/f/fridask01.shtml
[218] http://www.baseball-reference.com/boxes/NYA/NYA192307020.shtml
[219] http://www.baseball-reference.com/boxes/NYA/NYA192307030.shtml
[220] http://www.baseball-reference.com/boxes/NYA/NYA192307041.shtml

at 45,000. Herb Pennock and Paul Zahniser were pitching. The Yanks knocked Zahniser out by early in the third inning, including two home runs. Hollingsworth came in relief and finished the game. He gave up five hits and three runs. Final score: 12-6, Yankees win.

**Game 4: July 4 Yankee Stadium 1: Game 2:**[221] It would seem that if Cy Warmoth were healthy, and his past successes against the Yankees considered, he would have earned a start. Instead Bush sent in Walter Johnson who had been murdered earlier in a relief attempt. No doubt the Big Train was hurting for revenge . . . and maybe just hurting. He was having a slow, if not bad, season. Whatever the reason the result was the same. Johnson faced 12 batters and gave up eight hits and six runs. Yankee catcher Fred Hoffman nailed him for a home run. Donie Bush yanked Walter Johnson and sent in Cy during the second inning. Cy fared not much better. He allowed nine hits, gave up two walks and let six runs score. The Yankees won 12-2.

It is interesting to compare the results of the Yankees game comparing the three pitchers in it. Sad Sam Jones was pitching for the Yanks in game 2 and he pitched all nine innings unassisted.

It is worth noting that a newly acquired Yankee rookie had been sidelined for this series. He had hit in most of the games he played. Some of the sportswriters thought he had great potential. His name was Lou Gehrig.

| Name of Pitcher | IP | BF | Hits | Walks | Strike Outs | HR Allowed | Runs | ERA |
|---|---|---|---|---|---|---|---|---|
| **New York Yankees** | | | | | | | | |
| Sad Sam Jones | 9 | 39 | 8 | 2 | 4 | 0 | 2 | 2.88 |
| **Washington Nationals** | | | | | | | | |
| Walter Johnson | 1.1 | 12 | 8 | 0 | 1 | 1 | 6 | 4.00 |
| Cy Warmoth | 6.2 | 31 | 9 | 2 | 7 | 1 | 2 | 4.22 |

There is no question that Sad Sam Jones was the dominant pitcher. The Yankees won the game 12-2. Cy's numbers and those of Johnson are amazingly similar. Cy faced 19 more batters than Johnson. They each allowed

---

[221] http://www.baseball-reference.com/boxes/NYA/NYA192307042.shtml

a home run. Cy struck out nearly eighteen percent of the batters he faced. Johnson had an 8.33 strikeout percentage. Jones gave up eight hits during the game. Johnson and Warmoth allowed a combined total of 17 hits.

Cy Warmoth struck out seven Yankees. This is not something an ailing pitcher would normally accomplish. While no one understood it on July 4, 1923 this Yankees team mercilessly beating the Nationals was one of the great teams. They would go on to win the World Series in six games, defeating the feared and legendary New York Giants. The Yankees scored 823 runs and allowed their opponents to score only 622. The Yankees record for 1923 would be 98-54. This team won nearly 65 percent of its games.

Undoubtedly there were fireworks following the Yankees win in the City of New York. There must have also been fireworks inside the Nationals organization. For reasons unknown, this was (almost) Cy's last game in Major League Baseball. He was on his way south. It must have been a bittersweet journey. Cy was traded to the Memphis Chickasaws.

Cy went south as ordered.

Then Fall fell upon Memphis and something quite peculiar happened. The Nationals wanted Cy back on their team. President Griffith announced a "deal" had been made to borrow Cy back from the Memphis team. Cy Warmoth dutifully went back to Washington as required by his contract. Exactly what was happening inside the Nationals organization is uncertain and there are no visible records to give us the entire story. An article appeared in The Washington Post August 31, 1923 which sheds some light on the situation:

> "President Griffith of the Nationals last night announced that he had made a deal with the Memphis club whereby pitcher Wallace Warmoth will immediately leave to rejoin the Nats. In exchange Monroe Mitchell will be loaned to the Memphis Team to finish out the Southern Association season, after which he will be brought back here.
>
> "When Griffith was criticized for his action sometime ago in sending both Hollingsworth and Warmoth to Memphis in exchange for Mitchell, he stated that in his opinion, neither of the two let out by the Nats had the necessary qualifications to make good in the Johnson circuit and that he believed Mitchell to be a great prospect." (Article

purchased from Proquest Historical Newspaper and reprinted with permission.)

We gather several insights from this two paragraph story:

1. The decision to trade Cy was made by the club President Clark Griffith.
2. Someone convinced Griffith Mitchell was a hot prospect.
3. Griffith (and probably Donie Bush had a vote in it) did not think Cy Warmoth was good enough to compete on the American League level
4. He had given away both Warmoth and Hollingsworth to get Mitchell.
5. Griffith ate crow and brought Cy back.

Another question presents itself. Why did Griffith make the deal to begin with? The only answers we come up with are speculative. But looking at past history and dealings in other organizations we can give some possible answers:

1. Since it had no farm system of its own, the Nationals and other American League owners had been raiding the Southern Association for players. Memphis had a good team and Griffith may have been helping them by giving them two "big name" pitchers. This certainly would have helped the gate draw in Memphis and getting people into the ballpark was the only way the Chickasaw owners had to make money.
2. Scouts may have "over-sold" Griffith on Mitchell's abilities. He may have made a very bad deal which he regretted. It is unusual that he asked only to get Cy Warmoth back to finish the season. It is interesting to note the Nats were giving Mitchell back and there was no mention of his future return. Nor did Hollingsworth come back.
3. Cy was in Memphis long enough in 1923 to pitch 11 games. He won six and lost five. Mitchell, the hot prospect, won 2 and lost four and was finished as a major leaguer. In 1924 he and Cy would share duties on the pitching staff of the Memphis Chickasaws. It would seem Griffith was the loser in this deal. Yet, his team would

win the 1924 American Pennant and the World Series without help from Cy, Mitchell or Hollingsworth.

Cy's first return appearance was for one inning on **September 9, 1923** in a game against Philadelphia in Griffith Stadium. He struck out one of three batters he faced and allowed no hits and no runs. The Athletics won 5-2 and Tom Zachary was the losing pitcher.[222]

**September 15, 1923:** Cy returned to the mound as a starter. He pitched only two innings, faced nine batters, allowing three hits and one walk before being pulled by Bush. Paul Zahniser followed Cy giving up seven runs and Firpo Marberry relieved him and allowed one more run. The Nationals were down 8-2 when the Nationals staged yet another last inning rally, scoring seven runs. Cy was yet again declared the winning pitcher. His record improved to 7-5.[223] His lifetime record was 8-5. In winning, Cy also saw the new hope for the Nationals. Marberry would be a "saver" for Washington. In the coming year he would save 15 games for the Nationals and help propel them to their first world series victory. In his career he would win 148 games with 101 saves.[224]

**Monday, September 17, 1923, Griffith Stadium:** Cy battled once more against the titanic St. Louis Browns on this unusual day in baseball. The Browns were in Washington. Walter Johnson was given starts in both games of a double header. (Was this an attempt to get The Big Train closer to a 20-game mark?) Johnson started game one and pitched three innings. He then turned the game over to Cy who pitched five innings, giving up six hits and four runs. Firpo Marberry then came in and completed the game. The Nationals won 5-4 and Walter Johnson got credit for the win.[225]
**Game 2:** The Big Train started and finished this game without relief. He actually pitched seven innings. He allowed only six hits and two runs. The Nationals won 12-2. Now the Nationals were only 2-1/2 games out of fourth spot in the American League. Fourth was now held by the team with whom they had been playing, the St. Louis Browns. It had been a banner day, Walter Johnson won two games and the Nationals were moving up in the League. It was for naught, however, Tom Zachary pitched the next to the last game of the series the very next day and lost it 5-1. George Mogridge,

---

[222] http://www.baseball-reference.com/boxes/WS1/WS1192309090.shtml
[223] http://www.baseball-reference.com/boxes/WS1/WS1192309150.shtml
[224] http://www.baseball-reference.com/players/m/marbefi01.shtml
[225] http://www.baseball-reference.com/boxes/WS1/WS1192309171.shtml

who was now pitching better than ever, came back for the last game and pitched a nine-hit shutout. The Browns left Washington only a game and one-half ahead of the Nationals.[226] Cy was probably happy to help Walter get two wins in one day but this effort was not record worthy. More than 30 pitchers pitched *complete 9-inning games* back-to-back doubleheaders and won both in the early years years of baseball. Joe McGinnity of the New York Giants did it three times in 1906.

**October 3, 1923 Shibe Park, Philadelphia:** This would be the last time Cy appeared in Major League Baseball as a pitcher. The start was given to yet another young man recruited by Griffith from the Southern Association. James "Clay" Shad Roe, a 19-year old native of Tennessee who rose to attention in the Cotton League (pitching for the Vicksburg Hill Billies), had gained Nationals attention pitching for the Chattanooga Lookouts. Griffith had brought him in for a look. His Major League career lasted one game. It measured not quite two innings. Cy relieved him in the second inning and faced the next 26 batters. He allowed five runs on six hits.

In yet another turn of irony, Cy was replaced by a young man named Fred "Buck" Shemankske who had also been called up on trial. The young man, born in Detroit, was brought up from the Evansville Evas, a team from which Cy too had advanced his climb into the majors. This would be the only Major League Baseball game Shemankske would ever pitch. He gave up six hits and three runs before ending the game. The Nationals lost 12-8. Roe was given the loss.[227]

On October 4 at Griffith Stadium Paul Zahniser ended his season 9-10 with a loss to the Boston Red Sox.

On October 5 in the first game of a double header Walter Johnson ended his season with a 4-2 win over the Sox. He ended 1923 with a 17-12 record.

October 5 in the second game, Firpo Marberry got his fourth win against no losses on the season. The Nationals defeated the Sox 9-4.

In the last game of the season on October 7 at Griffith Stadium, the Nationals again defeated the Red Sox 5-2. George Mogridge again went the distance raising his record to 13-13.

---

[226] http://www.baseball-reference.com/boxes/WS1/WS1192309172.shtml
[227] http://www.baseball-reference.com/boxes/PHA/PHA192310030.shtml

The game produced a minor miracle. The Nationals had finished fourth in the American League with a 75-78 record. They finished 38 games behind the World Series champion Yankees.

Hardly anyone alive would have guessed that in just one year the Washington Nationals, in an exciting seventh game finish, provided by the Big Train Walter Johnson, would become the 1924 World Series Champions.

Cy would not be there. He would however have several more glimpses of glory ahead of him. in the minor leagues.

The Washington Senators/Nationals are a storied franchise. The butt of Vaudeville and other jokes for years, they finally gained their deserved respect with the 1924 win in the World Series. They returned to the World Series in 1925 but lost four games to three. In 1933 they lost four games to one. The franchise moved to Minnesota and became the Twins in 1961, breaking the hearts of Washingtonians. Under the banner of the Twins they also won World championships in 1987 (beating the St. Louis Cardinals) and 1991 (beating Atlanta). They also lost the World Series 4-2 to the Los Angeles Dodgers in 1965. The franchise has won the American League Pennant six times in its history.

Cy Warmoth would be almost forgotten in Washington D.C. but he had played an important bit part in the rise of the franchise from pauper to prince. His lifetime record was 8-5 (.615) and his lifetime ERA was 4.26. He pitched in 29 games and started 14. He pitched 129 innings of major league baseball. In his majors career he allowed 130 hits but gave up only four home runs. He passed 89 batters and struck out 54. He was called for a balk one time and cited for one wild pitch. That is the summary of his major league career.

# CHAPTER 12

# Way Down South In Dixie

## 1924

IT MIGHT SEEM being relegated to the minor leagues after having tasted the majors would be a devastating life-changing event. As the old poem said: "No it ain't necessarily so." Baseball was big business, in America. The minor leagues were a thriving bastion of free enterprise. Opportunity (although not necessarily lucrative for players) was everywhere in baseball. It was even possible to buy your own team or become manager of a thriving team. If you were a player who'd had your ticket punched in the major leagues, your chances were even better. Many players preferred the minors to the majors because they could maintain a semblance of family life. The major leagues, after all, weren't that good to their people. With the exception of a few teams such as the Yankees, players were still expected to share beds and travel in dirty old team cars rented by the owners. In many cases players had to do their own laundry

For these and other reasons, many smaller cities thrived with minor league activity. Memphis, Tennessee was a perfect example of being a great place to play baseball. The people of the Memphis area loved their Chickasaws just as much as fans in the big cities loved their major league teams. Attending a Southern Association League game was affordable, easy to do. and socially acceptable. What happened in a game would be talked about incessantly (at least until the next game). The players were not regarded as kings but dukes and princes when the team was winning and bums when they were losing. They ate at local diners and lived in the community rooming houses. After all, these were the roaring twenties and America was thriving. When the season ended a lot of local businesses would find their players jobs to sustain them until the spring. But most of all there was the pride of saying you knew someone who had frolicked in the world's biggest playgrounds and knew other men who were truly Gods of sport. If Cy Warmoth told someone that he struck out Babe Ruth, he would be only a rung or two below Charlie Chaplin or William Randolph

Hearst. Babe Ruth was always at the top. Cy probably got free meals and coffees just by telling stories in those country diners.

No wonder the "Chicks" fans loved their team. One look at the 1924 roster and you see they were talent laden. When Cy looked at the roster he saw men he already knew through the baseball fraternity network. He had participated with or against them in baseball skirmishes held in dozens of ballparks across America. There were a dozen or more former major leaguers on the Chick's roster. Several were former Nationals. They included Slim McGrew, Rip Wade (who'd provided Cy with a game winning home run) and that upstart young pitcher Monroe Mitchell.

The local stars of the team had hardly any major league credits at all. Third Baseman Doc Protho, a local dentist, pulled a few game stints for the Nationals in 1920 and 1923 but his stardom would climb higher before his career ended. Johnny Dobbs, the coach, was becoming a beloved figure in Memphis. A Chattanooga boy, Dobbs ended his professional playing career in 1905 after five seasons and 582 games, at age 30. In 1907 he got a job managing the Nashville Volunteers. He had been managing in the Southern Association ever since. After Nashville there were two more years in Chattanooga governing the Lookouts. Next he entered a three-year stint in Montgomery, Alabama leading the Rebels. In 1914 he moved to New Orleans for a nine-season job managing the Pelicans. Now he was in Memphis. Wherever he went, scouts followed. He produced many Major League players.

Dobbs' 1924 team had a little trouble gelling. They lost three of their first five games and then erupted into domination of the league. After that they shifted into high gear and won most of the games they played. They had won 104 games at the end of the season.

Cy and another Illinois native Otto Merz (Redbud, Illinois) were both 20 game winners. Merz won 20 and lost six. Cy won 20 and lost 11. Merz was 35 and Cy was 31. They were two of the three oldest players on the team. The Memphis team won the race in the Southern Association over Atlanta by five games.

The team then went on to play in the Dixie Series. The Dixie Series pitted the winner of the Southern Association against the winner of the Texas Leagues. In the 1924 Dixie Series championships the Chicks lost to Fort Worth 4 games to three.

**The 1924 Memphis Chickasaws were rated as number 48 in the top 100 minor leagues of all time.**[228] Only one other team had scored as many wins as they did in the Southern Association. That team was the 1921 Memphis Chickasaws. The two teams had almost none of the same players or the same coach and yet the results were nearly identical. But, there is an interesting sidebar to the story:

The 1924 Fort Worth (Texas) Panthers were not an average team. Minor League Baseball has it rated as the fourth best of the top 100 teams in minor league baseball of all time. They had a plentitude of talent including a first baseman by the name of Clarence Otto "Big Boy" Kraft. Kraft was a "Babe Ruth" figure in minor league uniform. In fact, he almost broke Babe Ruth's record of home runs. He fell short of Babe's Major League Accomplishment of 59 homers but connected for his 55th home run in the last game (second game of a double header) in the 1924 season. The previous home run record in the minor leagues was 49 and Kraft's record (55) lasted for 32 years. Kraft held other records and some of them still stand. He was a talented hitter and in spite of his size (six foot 195 pounds) a formidable base runner. He is said to have hit a home run in his home ball park that measured over 650-feet

We know now that Cy made a contribution to Kraft's home run binge. In Journal 29 of the Society of America Baseball Research an unidentified author left us this summary:

> ". . . Only two players have ever hit three home runs in a single World Series game. Babe Ruth did it twice, in 1926 and 1928. Reggie Jackson did it on three swings in 1977. But these were not the first times it happened in the post-season, or the last. Clarence "Big Boy" Kraft of the Fort Worth Panthers smashed home runs in the first, third and fifth innings off Memphis pitcher Cy Warmoth in Game 5 of the 1924 Dixie Series. Kraft, a converted pitcher (like Ruth), was not much of a slugger (unlike Ruth) until the 1921 season. At age thirty-four he went on a power binge, hitting 31, 32, 32, and 55 home runs in consecutive seasons. His big season was 1924, when he set the Texas League record (since broken) with 55 home runs and the still-standing TL standard with 196 RBIs. It was a big finish for Big Boy, as he retired following the 1924 season to tend to his automobile business."

---

[228] http://www.minorleaguebaseball.com/milb/history/top100.jsp

Cy, of course, pitched on the Evansville Evas, the team that succeeded the Evansville River Rats. After playing a single game for the River Rats, Kraft went to play for a Class D team, the McLeansboro,(Illinois) Merchants. Shortly after his arrival the five-team league folded and McLeansboro moved to the Kentucky, Illinois, and Tennessee League. It was commonly known as the Kitty League. He next went to a team in Flint, Michigan. Kraft got to the majors in 1914 and played only three games for the Boston Braves and from there found his way to minor league baseball immortality in Texas. Kraft was a converted ex pitcher who came alive as a hitter after the so-called "lively" ball was introduced into baseball. He had no great major league credentials but life was so good in the Texas Leagues, who needed the majors?[229]

The Dixie Series was one of two post-season playoffs prestigious enough to merit being considered a minor league world series. The other huge one was the annual face off between the American Association and the International League and was called: "The Junior World Series."

---

[229] http://www.minorleaguebaseball.com/milb/history/top100.jsp?idx=4

# CHAPTER 13

# Memphis, Atlanta

## 1925-1926

IT WAS MENTIONED earlier that the main way ballparks had to make money was to sell tickets to ballgames and refreshments to the fans. There was another way, however. When cash flow was down owners could always sell their better players. Good players meant ready cash for both minor and major league team owners. Cy, fresh off his most successful season ever in baseball, suddenly found he was no longer the only left hander on the pitching staff. His old teammate and rival from the Washington Nationals, Jim Brillheart, was now on the Memphis team. Cy was soon sold.

Brillheart, who like Cy had helped get the Nationals to fourth place in the American League, had also missed the Nationals' 1924 World Series winning season. Brillheart had been traded, or sold we're not sure which, to the Richmond Colts, of the Virginia League. Brillheart, like Cy, had a banner season in 1924 winning 22 games while losing 14. The Colts were fourth of six teams in the "B" League.

The team records for the Southern Association are not published. Perhaps they will be in the future. We cannot tell how long Cy pitched for each team. Both Atlanta and Memphis show him with a 15-13 won/loss record and having pitched in 39 games. This is probably a combined total and his contributions per team cannot be deciphered. What is known is that Atlanta, which would have been the last team he hurled for in 1925, won the Southern Association championship.

Monroe Mitchell, the other Washington pitcher, for reasons unknown, had dropped out of professional baseball. He would reappear in 1926 in the Eastern League.

John Dobbs, the Southern Association's super winning coach, left Memphis for a five-year stint with the Birmingham Barons. In his place appeared a ghost from Cy's past. Clyde "Deer Foot" Milan was the new coach of the Chickasaws. It was Milan who had given Cy the assignment to pitch against the Yankees in 1922. Milan had been replaced by Donie Bush in 1923. Donie Bush, only one year into the Nationals job, had been replaced by Bucky Harris in 1924. Bush was establishing a pattern. Players often disliked his strong-handed tactics. He would managed many teams but not for long. Meanwhile, Cy was packing his bags again. He had been sold or traded to Atlanta.

The Atlanta Crackers, a wealthy team as minor league teams go, had been owned by a variety of owners including Coca-Cola™. The Crackers had just hired as coach one of the most remarkable men in baseball. Bert Niehoff had only six years of minor league baseball experience when he appeared on the field (third base) for the Cincinnati Reds in 1913. He played in only two games that year. In 1914 he returned to the Reds and played in 154 games. He switched to the Philadelphia Phillies in 1916 and led the National league in double plays. He left the majors in 1918 after playing 28 games for the St. Louis Cardinals and The New York Giants. He played in 581 regular season games and played in five games in the 1915 World Series for the Phillies who lost the series to Boston in five games. In 1919 he returned to minor league ball, playing for teams in the Pacific League. He also did a two-year stint for the Los Angeles Angels. Then in 1922 he landed a job as player manager for the Mobile Bears. After two years he moved to Atlanta. His career would last until 1954 when he was 70 years old. His minor league manager-player days ended in 1928 after 2,219 games. He hung up his spikes at age 44.[230]

Cy joined Niehoff and his team in yet another drive to the Dixie championship. Cy was one of 14 ex-Major Leaguers on the Atlanta team. They dominated the Southern Association and won the league title. They also earned the right to play in the Dixie. Just like the Memphis team the year before they had to confront the Fort Worth Panthers, one of the most successful franchises in Minor League History. The Panthers were coached by Jake Atz, another of the most successful minor league coaches ever. He also had 20 players who were coming/going to the majors. The Crackers lost the series to the Panthers by losing four out of six games.

Just keep in mind that Cy had now twice been to the closest thing the minor leagues had to a world series. We are uncertain how he performed there but the indications are that he did well. Well enough that a third team that wanted to go for the Dixie roses hired him away from the Atlanta Crackers. Cy was going to become a New Orleans Pelican.

---

[230] http://www.baseball-reference.com/players/n/niehobe01.shtml

# CHAPTER 14

# New Orleans, Kansas City

## 1927-1928-1929-1930

CY PLAYED FOR two teams in 1927. How and when he joined those two teams is not exactly known.

New Orleans was a city that bristled with baseball activity, especially in the spring. Two teams took New Orleans center stage in 1922, The Boston Red Sox and the New Orleans Pelicans. Several African American teams were also bustling around the city.

The Red Sox took Spring Training in New Orleans in 1926. If Cy reported to work early, he would have found a number of old combatants and comrades at the New Orleans Ball Park. Among them would been Baby Doll Jacobson, Fred Haney, Slim Harriss, and Paul Zahniser.

It was customary, in baseball's early years of Spring training, for the local teams to participate in exhibition games against the visiting major leaguers. Such a meeting between the Pelicans and the Red Sox probably happened in New Orleans in 1922 but we found no record of it.

Baseball was segregated. There *must not be*, by the dictates of professional baseball player-team contracts, *no participation in unauthorized exhibition games*. Games between professional white baseball players and members of black baseball teams were forbidden by spoken edict, if not written. In most cities blacks could pay and get into white professional ball games but they had to sit in sections reserved for people of color. Even in Washington and New York, melting pots of diversity, segregation was enforced.

Yet, there was another openly known secret. White ballplayers liked to watch their black counterparts and they occasionally sneaked into exhibition games under assumed names to test their skills against them. White players knew some of the African-American players were the best of the day. Joe DiMaggio and Dizzy Dean are known to have tried to outwit the great pitcher and future Hall of Fame member Satchel Paige in the 1930's. Dizzy Dean, baseball's most accomplished country color commentator supposedly once said of himself:

"Anybody who's ever had the privilege of seeing me play knows that I am the greatest pitcher in the world."

His tune changed after facing Leroy Robert "Satchel" Paige. Two more quotes attest to his revised found feelings.

1. "I know who's the best pitcher I ever see and it's old Satchel Paige, that big lanky colored boy. My fastball looks like a change of pace alongside that little pistol bullet ole Satchel (Paige) shoots up to the plate."
2. "If Satch (Paige) and I were pitching on the same team, we would clinch the pennant by July fourth and go fishing until World Series time."[231]

Joe DiMaggio also admitted having tested Satchel Paige in his minor league days and is reported to have said in reminiscence:

"After I got that hit off Satchel (Paige), I knew I was ready for the big leagues."[232]

Baseball was not finally integrated until 1947 and the player chosen to break the system was a young war veteran named Jackie Robinson. He was chosen as much for his disposition as for his ability. Owners knew the first man to break the color barrier would be required to take a lot of verbal abuse from both fans and opposing players. Satchel Paige finally got his chance to pitch in the white leagues a year later. While no one was really sure of his age, including himself, he was listed as being 41 years old his rookie year of 1948. He signed with the Cleveland Indians as a free agent. Later he played for the St. Louis Browns. Paige would pitch in five seasons and then retire from the majors. In 1965 he came back to pitch three innings for the Kansas City Athletics and got a save for his team. He was elected to the Major League Hall of Fame in 1971. He died and was buried in Kansas City June 8, 1982.

African Americans first organized teams and leagues of their own in the 1800's. Like the white teams, some failed but several were successful and made money for their owners. In many major league cities they provided money sorely needed by baseball team owners to improve their profit margins by playing their games in major league stadiums when the white teams were off or out of town. The Pittsburgh Grays, a team which featured Satchel Paige as a pitcher and a bone-crushing hitter named Josh Gibson could

---

[231] http://www.baseball-almanac.com/quotes/quodean.shtml
[232] http://www.baseball-almanac.com/quotes/quopaig.shtml

often not find room to house their crowds in Pittsburgh. They had at one time used Griffith Stadium in Washington, D.C. as their home stadium and often sold it out. They were so popular that many other major league teams invited them to their stadiums for Negro League and exhibition games.

New Orleans was a booming place in 1926. Things were looking even better for economic growth because the U.S. Army Corps of Engineers had just completed constructing a levy system around New Orleans and up the Mississippi River that practically guaranteed, they boasted, there would be no future flooding in that city.

There was another city where African American Baseball was thriving. It was Kansas City and Cy would pitch in both cities before 1926 had ended. Cy pitched 11 games in New Orleans and lost seven of them. He pitched 129 innings and had a respectable ERA of 3.35. He did, however, issue a lot of walks. His records indicate that he passed 75 batters and committed 48 errors in 11 games. Quite frankly the records seem suspect. Maybe he wanted to play somewhere else, or perhaps he had a really sore arm. For whatever reason, Cy was soon on his way to join the Kansas City Blues.[233]

Had Cy been able to stay in New Orleans he would have earned another trip to Dallas to take on the Fort Worth Panthers. They would lose but had Cy gone he would have been one of very few players to appear in three minor league "World Series" events. Fortunately that was not the end of his baseball story.

By this time in his career Cy Warmoth should have learned to appreciate barbeque and jazz as his career wound through Memphis, Atlanta, New Orleans and now Kansas City. In Kansas City, Missouri he was experiencing the roots of the American League. The Kansas City Blues were one of the original eight-member American Association. It was this league that Ban Johnson had parleyed into the American League.

Unfortunately there are not many records of Cy's performances in Kansas City. Baseball-Reference.com shows him pitching in only nine games in Kansas City in 1926. So Cy may have stayed with New Orleans longer than the records indicate. (The published records are incomplete. The Southern Association teams played a long schedule and played at least 156 games.)

In 1927 he is shown as having pitched in 11 games (81 innings total) with an ERA of 5.22. The same report says he walked 41 batters. His entire

---

[233] http://www.baseball-reference.com/minors/team.cgi?id=26414

career passing batters on balls had been a problem but the percentages here seem especially high. He is listed as 6-5 on the year.

His 1928 numbers, while larger, go negative on the win-loss scale. He is shown as winning 10 and losing 16. His ERA improved to 3.55. Jimmy Zinn, a 34-year old, five-season former major leaguer seems to have been the top pitcher for the Blues. Zinn had a 13-16 record pitching for the Pirates and one season for the Indians. Zinn's 1928 record for the Blues was 23-13 and his ERA was 3.48. Zinn pitched 323 innings. Cy pitched .218. One outfielder, Fred Nicholson, a former Pirate, Tiger and Boston Braves player, was shown playing in 167 games for the Blues. The Blues 1927 roster showed at least 26 players that had been or were going to the big show. Probably the biggest names on the list were Carl Hubbell, Bill Wambsganss, Dixie Davis and Red Oldham.

Cy appears to have been one of two left-handed pitchers on Manager Dutch Zwilling's 1927 staff. The other was a 24-year-old by the name of Carl "Meal Ticket" Hubbell. Hubbell would go on to a dynamic pitching career with the New York Giants. He would be inducted into the Baseball Hall of Fame in 1947. Manager Zwilling was famous on two counts in professional baseball. (1) He was the top homerun hitter in the ill-fated Federal League. (2) He is the alphabetically last in all of Major League Baseball. It appears he also had a preference for right handed pitchers. Now we come to one of the most exciting years in Cy Warmoth's professional career: 1929.

Whatever seemed to have afflicted Cy had passed in 1929. The Blues' talented bull pen of ten, seven of whom would or had been major league pitchers, would dominate the American Association. The hurling force would be led by Tom Clancy Sheehan, Max Thomas, Robert Murray, Lynn Nelson, Clyde Day and Cy.

Thomas (18-11) and Murray (17-8) are mysterious figures with no obvious major league pedigrees. Thomas hailed from Utah and Murray's origins and credentials are unknown. Either one, or both, of them could have been a southpaw. It seems unlikely the team would have only one left-hander for a pitcher. Thomas went on to have a long career in the minors. He is known to have pitched 376 games for teams in the American Association, Western League, Texas League and Pacific Coast League. He won 189 of those games. Murray appeared in 1929 and won 17 games while losing eight. He won two more games for Kansas City in 1930 then he disappears. He may have also played in the small town of Reading,

Illinois. Whatever the full story of these two minor league professionals, they certainly propelled the Blues to championships in 1929.

The other pitchers and their records were:

1. **Tom Sheehan**, 35, who went 16-11 for the Blues. He appeared in the majors six seasons and accumulated a 17-39 record. He made one appearance for the Yankees but played two seasons each for Philadelphia, Cincinnati and Pittsburgh. (He continued on into managing and in 1960 managed for the San Francisco Giants on a team that included Orlando Cepeda and Willie Mays.)
2. **Lynn Nelson**, 24, won 15 and lost six games for the Blues. He was one of the few pitchers on the Blues who was on his way up. He would get his first shows for the majors in 1930 and stay there for seven seasons. He would play three years for the Cubs and four years for the Athletics. His major league record would be 33-42. He would return to the minors and stay until 1943.
3. **Clyde "Pea Ridge" Day**, 29, contributed 12 wins and five losses to the Blues and had a 2.98 ERA. He had a 5-7 record in the major leagues. Ridge, a native of Pea Ridge, Arkansas, was one of the more colorful characters of baseball history. He was known for making hog calls from the pitcher's mound. He ceased to make the calls after taunting Babe Ruth when he got ahead of him in a game. Ruth laughed at his comical behavior and then sailed one of the park. Day also made short appearances for the Cardinals and Cincinnati Reds.
4. One of the old baseball names on the Blues was **Frank "Dixie" Davis.** Davis went 12-5 for the Blues in 1929. Davis played in the majors in 1912-1926 and left with a 75-71 record, playing most of his time with the dead ball. He had been on the St. Louis Browns teams Cy pitched to in 1922 and 1923. He spent 13 years in the minors.
5. Young **Blue Fette**[234], 22, was a Blues Pitcher on his way up the ladder and won seven games and lost only three in his 1929 effort. He would go 41-40 in the majors playing for the short-lived Boston Bees and finally the Brooklyn Dodgers in 1940. Fette would make it to the All Star game in 1939 as a National League reserve pitcher. He would pitch two innings

---

[234] http://www.baseball-reference.com/players/f/fettelo01.shtml

and strike out one batter and allow one hit and one walk. The majestic Joe DiMaggio would foul out on one of his pitches. He would also cause Hank Greenberg to ground out.[235]

6. **Johnny Morrison**, 35, was the only pitcher on the Blues Team who had pitched in the World Series. He pitched three innings in game seven of the 1925 series in what were probably the worst conditions ever encountered for a World Series game. He also played in game one and game four. His major league career spanned ten seasons and he rolled up a respectable record of 103-80. Morrison contributed three wins and two losses for Blues in the 1929 season.

7. **Dennis Burns** had a 1-1 record for the Blues in 1929. He also played for Beaumont in the Texas League during the same period where he went 16-13. He had a 9-10 record pitching for Philadelphia in 1923, 1924

It should be noted that it took a lot of pitchers to maintain a 170-game schedule.

So how did Cy help the team? Cy, at age 36, and Dixie Davis, 38, were the old men of the team. You learn a lot of baseball in 13 seasons of professional ball and surely his experiences were valuable to younger players. He also brought a strong and talented left arm that won 14 games and lost only four. But the won and lost stats didn't tell the whole story. Cy was showing remarkable talent in the 1929 season, even for an old gent. He appeared in 27 games and pitched 176 innings of baseball. There are no figures to show any saves he might have had. He was a contributor and nowhere was it more evident than this year when Cy and the Kansas City Blues earned the right to play in the real Junior World Series, a nine-game playoff between themselves and the Rochester, New York Red Wings of the International League.

It was more than just an honor for Cy, who had come precariously close to being in a Major League World Series. This was his third time to participate in a major minor league playoff. Few baseball players ever achieved that honor. If there EVER is a minor league Hall of Fame, this would almost surely win Cy a nomination.

The International League was composed of these teams in 1929 (alphabetical order) were:

---

[235] http://www.baseball-reference.com/boxes/ALS/ALS193907110.shtml

1. Baltimore (MD) Orioles
2. Buffalo (NY) Bisons
3. Jersey City (NJ) Skeeters
4. Montreal (CAN) Royals
5. Newark (NJ) Bears
6. Reading (PA) Keystones
7. Rochester (NY) Redwings
8. Toronto (CAN) Mapleleafs.

Only two of the teams had formal associations with Major League Baseball. Reading was a Chicago White Sox affiliate and the Red Wings were betrothed to the St. Louis Cardinals. (Incidentally all these teams had major followings. It was estimated that more than a quarter of a million fans paid to get into the Kansas City games.)

The American Association was made up of these teams:

1. Columbus (OH) Nationals
2. Indianapolis (IN) Indians
3. Kansas City (MO) Blues
4. Louisville (KY) Colonels
5. Milwaukee (WI) Brewers
6. Minneapolis (MN) Millers
7. St. Paul (MN) Saints
8. Toledo (Ohio) Mud Hens

None of the AA teams had affiliations with major league teams. It is worth noting that the manager for the Toledo Mud Hens in 1929 was a brilliant young (38) upcoming tactician by the name of Casey Stengel. Another interesting tidbit is that the Redwing's 36-year-old coach, Billy Southworth, was just beginning a new career path. He would one day be a manager for the St. Louis Cardinals and the Boston Braves. In 2008 he was inducted into the Baseball Hall of Fame.

The Kansas City Blues hosted the first four games of the Junior World Series and won three of the first four games. The series then moved to Rochester, which had won their stiffly competitive league by eleven games. The Blues had won their division by finishing 8 ½ games ahead of the St. Paul Saints. The Red Wings won the first two games played in Rochester which tied the series at three games each. The Blues won the seventh game of the series. The eighth game resulted in 5-5 tie and was called after 11 innings due to darkness. Kansas City won the game the next day with old Dixie Davis pitching on his birthday.

The Blues were Junior World Series Champions! Their team was rated as the 28th best team in Minor League History.

The story of the 1929 Junior World Series Champions is best described in a report for the Society of Baseball Research, exact author unknown. It gives a great summation of the team and Cy's part in it:

> "The 1929 Blues played winning baseball the entire season. Only once did the team lose as many as four games in a row and that slight setback was followed by a nine-game winning streak. Their main competition was a fine St. Paul club, but Kansas City took over first place to stay on June 19. The Blues clinched the pennant with one week remaining in the schedule and finally finished 8-½ games ahead of the Saints with a sparkling 111-56, .665 record—one of the best marks in American Association history. Kansas City led the league in only one offensive category, team triples (103). They were second in batting and third in fielding, but their pitchers gave up fewer runs (766 in 170 games) than any other team. Four of the seven pitchers with the lowest ERAs were Blues. Kansas City also was the American Association box office champion with an attendance of 281,376, 84,000 more than runner-up St. Paul.
>
> "In the Junior World Series, Kansas City faced an outstanding Rochester team that won the International League pennant by 11 games. The first four games of the best-of-nine series were played in Kansas City and when the teams shifted to Rochester the Blues held a 3-1 margin. The Red Wings won the first two games at home to tie the series at three wins apiece. The Blues took game seven, the second win for Lynn Nelson. After a day off, the next contest wound up in a 5-5 tie, called by darkness at the end of 11 innings. The next afternoon, Rochester took an early 4-0 lead, but Kansas City fought back and after seven innings the score was tied 5-5, the same as the day before. This time, however, the Blues pushed across a run in the top of the 11th to lead 6-5. Veteran right-hander Dixie Davis, who had celebrated his 39th birthday the day before, shut the door on the Red Wings in the bottom of the 11th and Kansas City was the Junior World Series champion."[236]

---

[236] http://research.sabr.org/journals/index.php (then search Cy Warmoth)

1929 Kansas City Blues pitching statistics

| PITCHER | W | L | PCT | G | GS | CG | SH | SV | IP | H | BB | SO | ERA |
|---|---|---|---|---|---|---|---|---|---|---|---|---|---|
| Max Thomas | 18 | 11 | .621 | 50 | | | | | 231 | 210 | 88 | 82 | 3.11 |
| George Murray | 17 | 8 | .680 | 41 | | | | | 218 | 258 | 87 | 46 | 4.63 |
| Tom Sheehan | 16 | 11 | .593 | 37 | | | | | 243 | 257 | 59 | 74 | 3.78 |
| Lynn Nelson | 15 | 6 | .714 | 38 | | | | | 190 | 184 | 77 | 78 | 2.99 |
| Wallace Warmoth | 14 | 4 | .778 | 27 | | | | | 176 | 164 | 79 | 61 | 3.38 |
| Pea Ridge Day | 12 | 5 | .706 | 36 | | | | | 178 | 162 | 33 | 76 | 2.98 |
| Dixie Davis | 8 | 5 | .615 | 21 | | | | | 84 | 84 | 35 | 30 | 4.07 |
| Lou Fette | 7 | 3 | .700 | 46 | | | | | 154 | 171 | 71 | 43 | 4.33 |
| Dewey Morrison | 3 | 2 | .600 | 6 | | | | | 29 | 25 | 14 | 9 | |

Not long after the 1929 season ended, there was a life-changing event in America. The stock market crashed on October 29, 1929 sending life in America into a horrendous downwards spiral. The "Roaring Twenties" came to a painful end and there was no exemption for professional baseball. Even Babe Ruth would take multiple salary cuts. By 1934 his salary would be reduced by 75 percent.

The immediate and coordinated actions taken by major league baseball owners were to cut salaries, reduce expenses and limit training. They allowed each team to have only twenty three players on a team. Later on owners came up with some innovative things to spur interest in baseball. They introduced All Star games and created a Hall of Fame. They passionately fought two other suggested ideas. They said no to live radio broadcasts of regular season games and spurned suggestions the fields be lighted for night baseball. They were ideas which would rise again.

The second cardinal rule of baseball ownership was amplified. If you need cash, sell a really good player. Ironically an all time record of attendance was established for major league baseball in 1930. More than ten million people attended baseball games.[237] Attendance would steeply decline in 1932 when the federal government imposed a ten percent tax on baseball tickets. President Herbert Hoover was booed when he attended baseball games, a sport he dearly loved.

Cy kept his job in 1930. He would again pitch for the Kansas City Blues.[238]

Attendance at Kansas City Blues games suffered tremendously, nearly halving the previous season's record attendance. The Blues had nearly the same staff but fared not nearly so well. They were the second place team in the American Association. Cy won six games and lost seven. He pitched 126 innings. It was time to move again.

Before we follow Cy to his last baseball home, there is a tragic tale to tell about two of Cy's Bullpen friends on the 1929 team. The friends were Max Thomas and Pea Ridge Day, the hog-calling pitcher.

Henry Clyde Day, born in Center, Mo. in 1899, took some hard emotional shocks in his life. His fans never had a clue as they watched the comical figure giving the hog call from the pitchers mound and committing dozens of other outrageous acts. Baseball was his lifeblood and salvation.

---

[237] http://bss.sfsu.edu/tygiel/hist490/1930s/articles/out-13.pdf
[238] http://www.nytimes.com/2009/01/07/sports/baseball/07depression.html?_r=1&scp=5&sq=ken%20belson&st=cse

Pea Ridge, Arkansas is a small town nestled in the Ozarks in the upper northwest corner of Arkansas bordering Missouri. Pea Ridge is located in Benton County, a county named for U.S. Senator Thomas Hart Benton, instrumental in getting Arkansas admitted to statehood in 1826. A notable Civil War Battle was fought there in March of 1862. A national park was opened there in 1966. From the time of the battle until the Park opened, the community had little additional claim to fame.

One of the very most exciting things of the era was watching Henry Clyde Day rise to fame in baseball. He started out pitching professional baseball when he signed with the Joplin, Missouri Miners in 1923. Despite his personal eccentricities, he was recognized as a person of talent and potential. In 1924 he went to Muskogee, Oklahoma to pitch for another Class C team, the Athletics, and in September of that year he was invited to St. Louis to pitch for the Cardinals. The Cardinals started him in three games. He won one and lost one. In 1925 they brought Day back and used him in 17 games, letting him start four games. He won two games and lost four but had an exceptionally high ERA. The Cardinals sent him to Syracuse of the International League. After pitching at Syracuse, Day was signed by Cincinnati in 1926. In his short trial with the Reds, his ERA was still exceptionally high (7.36). He was sent back to the minors and played for the Los Angeles Angels, Wichita Larks and Omaha Crickets. By the time he came to Kansas he was a superb pitcher and in the championship series of 1929 had an ERA of 2.98.

Day's performance with the Blues was a ticket back to the majors. In 1931 he started pitching for the Brooklyn Robins. Day went 2-2 for the Robins with an ERA of 4.55. In 1932 he was back in the minor leagues and pitching for the Minneapolis Millers in the American Association.[239] Day's arm began to fail and he was released. He soon became despondent. In 1934, in the midst of the depression, he underwent special surgery costing more than $10,000 at the Mayo Clinic. The surgery failed to revive the arm. He began to drink heavily. He had a wife of 11 years pregnant with their first child when he traveled to Kansas City to have treatment for memory loss. While there he visited his old teammate and close friend Max Thomas. While talking with Thomas he became totally despondent, grabbed a hunting knife off a table and slit his own throat. Thomas tried to stop him but Day knocked him away.

---

[239] http://www.baseball-reference.com/players/ (Henry Clyde Day)

It was a terrible end to a man who had already known much tragedy. His brother, also a pitcher, had a leg amputated and died of blood poisoning in 1922. His mother committed suicide by ingesting poison in 1929 and his father died of a heart attack in 1934.[240]

Max Thomas pitched until he was 44 years old. He never played major league baseball. He pitched 669 games but he carried this horrid memory of Pea Ridge's end with him the rest of his days.

---

[240] http://en.wikipedia.org/wiki/Pea_Ridge_Day

# CHAPTER 15

# The 'Little Train' Stops in Omaha

IN 1931 AT age 38 Cy Warmoth's baseball train was rolling into its last stop. With America plunged deep in depression and millions unemployed, the refugees of the major leagues rolled into the minor leagues.

The Kansas City Blues picked up several refugees from the majors. The pitchers included Joe Dawson, a 27-year old reliever from the Pittsburgh Pirates who had started for the Blues back in 1922. They also picked up two right handers from the Cleveland Indians, Guy Morton, 31 and Jim Sullivan. Hank Thormahlen, 27, came up from Dallas in the Texas League to do left hand work. They were also fortunate to acquire the services of another lefty who was on his way up. Bill Walker, born in Belleville, Illinois in 1903 was working his way up the baseball ladder. He had played four games for Kansas City in 1924, pitching four and losing four. Walker was learning in the school of hard knocks. He also pitched a few games for Evansville, Indiana in 1925. Evansville's III League team was now the Pocketeers. The Pocketeers also played in Bosse Field, the nation's third oldest ballpark used for professional baseball. It was the same field where Cy had played on the Evansville Eva's team. (Only Fenway and Wrigley Field were in use earlier.) Walker was one of a long list of major league players who would spend time there. His career would accelerate in 1927 with a look from the New York Giants. Walker would spend his career there and win 97 games and lose 77 games. He would have eight saved games to his credit. His crown jewel would be pitching two games against Dizzy Dean and company in the 1934 season. Unfortunately he lost both games.

New pitchers coming to Kansas meant it was time for Cy to move on. For the first time in a long time he took a step down. Cy took a step downhill to play for the Omaha Packers in Nebraska. The Packers were members of the Western League Class A team. If the available records are correct, in 1931 at age 38 he played in six games for the Packers. He never started a game and left with a 2-2 record.

There comes a day when every athlete must quit the game, or the game quits him. This was the end of the line for Cy. There were no old friends to see his final fade. Pete Lapan, the catcher from the Nationals who had caught him when he destroyed the New York Yankees in 1922 had passed through Omaha, San Antonio and Birmingham the year before and was now doing his own dying swan song in Shreveport, Louisiana. There was only about eighteen month's difference in their ages. They had both had their glimpses of glory and were now being discharged into oblivion.

It was a good time to leave, the drought was beginning. Soon the midcontinent would be draped in dirt and darkness. The Dust Bowl days were on the horizon.

It might be argued that Cy was not really important to baseball. It could never be argued that baseball was not important to Cy. Even if you are not impressed by his pitching credentials or record, you have to admit that he saw professional baseball from the inside out when the game itself was just a kid. He knew many of the Gods of the game when they were clothed in dirty uniforms and tobacco drooled out the corners of their mouths.

Wallace Walter Warmoth took a journey in baseball which did not bestow the riches of a magnate or the jewels of a king. Nor did his fame spread across the globe. Yet Cy played the game in a quiet and exciting time in the history of the sport. At the end he shifted gears and went back to being an everyday citizen, dying without fanfare June 20, 1957. The Washington, D.C. Post and Times Herald ran this notice upon learning of his death.

## FORMER PITCHER DIES

MOUNT CARMEL, Ill., June 20 (A)—Wallace Warmoth, 64, pitcher for the Washington Senators during the late 1920s, died today. His wife, two sons and a daughter survive.

If Cy Warmoth found glory, it was probably in Baseball Heaven where the desire burning in the heart mattered more than the weight of the bat or the winding of the ball.

## Cy's Network of Notable Baseball Players

1. **Babe Ruth**, NY Yankees Opponent, Cy struck him out at least once One of first five members elected to **Baseball Hall of Fame. Top 100**
2. **Walter "Big Train" Johnson** Washington Senators Teammate Maybe the best AL pitcher ever. One of first five members elected to **Baseball Hall of Fame Top 100**
3. **Ty Cobb** Detroit Tigers Opponent Cy struck him out at least once. One of first five members elected to **Baseball Hall of Fame Top 100**
4. **George Sisler** St. Louis Browns Opponent (Sidelined when Cy pitched) Often referred to as "the perfect player" Voted into **Baseball Hall of Fame** 1939 **Top 100**
5. **Joe Sewell** Cleveland Indians, NY Yankees Cy 1st of only four pitchers to strike him out twice in one game Inducted into **Baseball Hall of Fame** 1977. One of most prolific hitters ever **Top 100**
6. **Tris Speaker** Boston Red Sox, Cleveland Indians et al (Player/Manager) Opponent Inducted **Baseball Hall of Fame 1937** (first of second class of inductees) **Top 100**
7. **Harry Heilman** Cleveland Indians Opponent Cy pitched him in several times in1923 Elected to **Baseball Hall of Fame** in 1937 **Top 100**
8. **Three-Fingered Mordecai Brown** Chicago Cubs, et al Opponent of Cy in 1920 Terre Haute Browns vs Evansville Evas Inducted into **Baseball Hall of Fame** in 1949 **Top 100**
9. **Travis Jackson** New York Giants He appeared in the 1934 All Star Game Cy's Teammate in Little Rock 1922 Elected to **Baseball Hall of Fame** in 1982
10. **Lou Gehrig** New York Yankees Opponent Sidelined as a Rookie when Cy pitched Inducted in **Baseball Hall of Fame** 1939 **Top 100**
11. **Bucky Harris** Washington Nationals, Detroit Tigers, et al Teammate 10 seasons Washington, 2 seasons Detroit ;(player/manager in Washington WS in 1924) Inducted as **Manager in Baseball Hall of Fame in 1975**
12. **Dazzy Vance** Brooklyn Robins Opponent in Minors Pages 49 **Elected to Baseball Hall of Fame** in 1955 **Top 100**

13. **Sam Rice** Washington Nationals, Teammate, inducted into **Baseball Hall of Fame** in 1963
14. **Goose Goslin** Washington Senators, et al Played in 32 World Series Games Teammate 1922-1923 Selected **Baseball Hall of Fame** 1968 Inducted in **Hall of Fame** in 1968 **Top 100**
15. **Rogers Hornsby** St. Louis Cardinals and others (et al) Teammate in 1916 Elected **Baseball Hall of Fame** 1942 **Top 100**
16. **Carl Hubbell** NY Giants Teammate in 1927 in Kansas City Elected to **Baseball Hall of Fame** in 1947 **Top 100**
17. **Miller Huggins** St. Louis Cardinals, New York Yankees Player Manager **Baseball Hall of Fame** Member Selected 1964
18. **Urban "Red" Faber** Chicago White Sox Opponent (last legal spitball pitcher) Opponent. Cy faced him in 1921 Elected to **Baseball Hall of Fame** in 1964
19. **Eddie Collins** Eddie Collins spent 25 years in the major leagues with the Philadelphia Athletics and Chicago White Sox, primarily at 2B Opponent **Baseball Hall of Fame** member inductee in 1939; played 34 games in seven world series 1914 MVP in AL **Top 100**
20. **Donie Bush** Spent 14 seasons with Ty Cobb and the Detroit Tigers. Managed for Washington first then Pittsburgh, White Sox and Reds Manager/Teammate baseball legend, nominated 6 times to Baseball Hall of Fame but never selected
21. **Roger Peckinpaugh** Opponent New York Yankees, Cleveland and White Sox. Played in more than 2, 000 games Teammate in 1922, 1923 9 nominations to Baseball Hall of Fame but never elected
22. **Ossie Bluege** Played 18 seasons at Washington, played more than 1, 860 games Teamate 1922, 1923 Played in three WS, nominated six times for Baseball Hall of Fame but never elected
23. **Muddy Ruel** Teammate Played more than 1450 games in 19 seasons. Opponent 1922, Teammate 1923 nominations to Baseball Hall of Fame but never elected
24. **Joe Judge** Played 17 seasons for Washington, 3 for others; teammate 1922-23, played more than 2, 080 games; 71 career home runs; lifetime BA .298 Teamate Played 14 games in

two WS; 7 nominations to Baseball Hall of Fame but never elected

25. **Red Lucas** Giants, Boston Braves, Pirates Nashville Teammate in 1921 Nominated three times to the Baseball Hall of Fame but never selected
26. **Urban Shocker** Yankeees and St. Louis Browns Opponent (66, 85, 104, 114) Won 187 games pitching and 25 saves; nominated for Hall of Fame but never selected. He went 24-17 in 1922.
27. **Eddie Foster** Washington, Boston, St. Louis Browns Opponent St. Louis Browns A regular on the hitting leader boards "at bats"; nominated to Baseball Hall of Fame in 1938, never elected.
28. **Baby Doll Jacobson,** St. Louis Browns, opponent, a real warrior on the diamond and rated one of the top 100 hitters of all time.
29. **Jimmy Dykes** Philadelphia Athletics, Chicago White Sox Opponent 19-time nominee to Baseball Hall of Fame, never elected;played 18 WS and two All Star Games
30. **Herb Pennock** Yankees, Boston Red Sox, Philadel-phia Athletics Opponent Inducted into **Baseball Hall of Fame** in 1948. One of the best AL pitchers ever; pitched 10 games in four WS.
31. **Stan "Covey"** Cleveland Indians, Washington, New York Yankees Opponent Elected to **Baseball Hall of Fame** in 1969; won 60% of the 357 games he pitched plus 21 saves
32. **Ray Schalk** Chicago White Sox, NY Giants Opponent Elected to **Baseball Hall of Fame** in 1955
33. **Billy Southworth** Cleveland Indians, Pittsburgh Pirates, Boston Braves, New York Giants, St. Louis Cardinals 1913-1929; Coached St. Louis Cardinals to 3 pennants and 2 World Championships 1943-1945. Elected to **Baseball Hall of Fame** as manager in 2008.

**1916 Cardinal Teammates:** Red Ames. Zinn Beck, Bob Bescher, Bruno Betzel, Sam Bohne, Tony Brotttem, Art Butler, Roy Corhan, Walton Cruise, Murphy Currie, Bill Doak, Mike Gonzalez, Dan Griner, Charley Hall, Rogers Hornsby, Miller Huggins, Hi Jasper, Tom Long, Joe Lotz, Lee Meadows, Dots

Miller, Slim Sallee, Jack Smith, Frank Snyder, Bob Steele, Stuffy Stewart, Milt Watson, Steamboat Williams, Chief Wilson.

**1923 Senators Teammates:** Ossie Bluege, Jim Brillheart, Donie Bush, Bill Conroy, Joe Evans, Showboat Fisher, Skipper Friday, Patsy Gharrity, Goose Goslin, Pinky Hargrave, Bucky Harris, Bonnie Hollingsworth, Walter Johnson, Joe Judge, Pete Lapan, Nemo Lebold, Firpo Marberry, Slim McGrew, Monroe Mitchell, George Mogridge, Bobby Murray, Jim O'Neill, Roger Peckinpaugh, Squire Potter, Jake Propst, Doc Protho, Sam Rice, Jim Riley, Clay Roe, Muddy Ruel, Allen Russell, Fred Schemanske, Duke Sedgwick, Carr Smith, Rip Wade, Ted Wingfield, Tom Zachary, Paul Zahniser.

\* \* \*

**AUTHORS NOTE: TOP 100** refers to players listed in **Lawrence Ritter and Donald Honig's** *The 100 Greatest Baseball Players of All-Time,* **Crown Publishers, Inc., New York 1981)**

Edwards Brothers Malloy
Thorofare, NJ USA
June 24, 2013